Uncovering Black Heroes

Peter Lang PRIMERS

in Education

Shirley R. Steinberg
General Editor

The Peter Lang Primers series is part of the Peter Lang Education list.
Every volume is peer reviewed and meets
the highest quality standards for content and production.

PETER LANG
New York • Bern • Frankfurt • Berlin
Brussels • Vienna • Oxford • Warsaw

David Boers

Uncovering Black Heroes

Lesser-Known Stories of
Liberty and Civil Rights

PETER LANG
New York • Bern • Frankfurt • Berlin
Brussels • Vienna • Oxford • Warsaw

Library of Congress Cataloging-in-Publication Data

Names: Boers, David, author.
Title: Uncovering Black heroes: lesser-known stories
of liberty and civil rights / David Boers.
Description: New York: Peter Lang Publishing, 2017.
Series: Peter Lang primers; vol. 37 | ISSN 2572-5831
Caroline Quarlls, Joshua Glover, National Association of
Colored Women's Clubs, Ezekiel Gillespie, James Groppi, Vel Phillips
Includes bibliographical references.
Identifiers: LCCN 2017002926 | ISBN 978-1-4331-4165-2 (paperback: alk. paper)
ISBN 978-1-4331-4171-3 (ebook pdf) | ISBN 978-1-4331-4172-0 (epub)
ISBN 978-1-4331-4173-7 (mobi)
Subjects: LSCH: African Americans—Biography.
Abolitionists—United States—Biography. | Abolitionists—Wisconsin—Biography.
Civil rights workers—United States—Biography.
Civil rights workers—Wisconsin—Biography.
African Americans—Suffrage—Case studies. | African Americans—Suffrage—Wisconsin.
National Association of Colored Women's Clubs (U.S.)
Classification: LCC E185.96 .B576 2017 | DDC 920.0092/96073—dc23
LC record available at https://lccn.loc.gov/2017002926
DOI 10.3726/b11000

Bibliographic information published by **Die Deutsche Nationalbibliothek**.
Die Deutsche Nationalbibliothek lists this publication in the "Deutsche
Nationalbibliografie"; detailed bibliographic data are available
on the Internet at http://dnb.d-nb.de/.

Cover design by Clear Point Designs

© 2017 Peter Lang Publishing, Inc., New York
29 Broadway, 18th floor, New York, NY 10006
www.peterlang.com

All rights reserved.
Reprint or reproduction, even partially, in all forms such as microfilm,
xerography, microfiche, microcard, and offset strictly prohibited.

DEDICATION

This book is dedicated to the millions of beautiful people of all ethnic and other backgrounds throughout the centuries who have been born with excitement, joy, and hope but whose social standing and life experiences have crushed their spirits, oppressed their lives, and ripped away their hope.

And to those courageous, selfless people who through overt and covert ways have done what they could do with what they had where they were to unlock the chains of oppression so that spirits would rise, hope would return, and justice could prevail.

And to those who will read these stories and decide themselves to see the inequities in present society and culture and, most importantly, to find thoughtful ways to equalize the living experiences for all human beings.

May progress be continued toward liberty and justice.

CONTENTS

Preface	ix
Acknowledgments	xi
Introduction: Why Are These Stories Important to Tell?	1
Chapter 1: St. Louis to Detroit	7
Chapter 2: Releasing Joshua Glover: Wisconsin's Response to Popular Sovereignty, States' Rights, and the Fugitive Slave Law	23
Chapter 3: The Birth of the National Association of Colored Women's Clubs	39
Chapter 4: Uncovering Ezekiel Gillespie: African American Male Suffrage	69
Chapter 5: Milwaukee Movers: James Groppi/Vel Phillips	81
Chapter 6: Attorney for the Plaintiffs: Desegregating Milwaukee Public Schools	101
Conclusion: What Have We Learned About Uncovering Lesser-Known Heroes?	117

Selected Court Decisions Regarding Discrimination
Based on Ethnicity   123

Selected Court Decisions Regarding Discrimination
Based on Gender   125

PREFACE

What is revealed in this book is the linkage between vastly unknown local events and personal actions and the recognized civil rights movements and leaders that are known widely on a national level. While events on a national scale trudge forward with diligence and courageous struggle so do lesser-known events that connect, feed into, and form the foundation of a national movement. The manuscript attempts to form the concept that national leaders made their gains only with the help of local agency. The essays/stories laid out as chapters in this book are real-life examples of the local backbone that helped the national efforts stand tall. Though usually with networks of support behind them, these local freedom fighters had much to lose and small chance of gain but they struck out in the dream of a better and more equal land. It is when their stories are brought to light that it becomes clear that national leaders were not acting alone and that local efforts were in play across the nation directly and indirectly in support of those who were more readily recognized.

The chapters presented should bring about a curiosity as to what history is present within the reader's locale and how that history connected with the greater movements for civil/social rights. This book will provide questions as to how local politics and social norms impacted the attempts by oppressed populations to gain a social, economic, and political foothold. From this, readers should begin to question the plights of local freedom fighters and their oppositional forces. They should thus then investigate how the opposition was faced and what the results of that were. The book should connect readers to more than just national movements and leaders; indeed, readers should become much more aware of how it takes more than a few national leaders to make a movement work and that without the courage and sacrifice of those not yet listed in history books progress toward social justice and equality might not have occurred. The chapters themselves are distinctive and unique in the depth of personal/historical detail of the events surrounding the actions of these particular courageous players in the quest for equality.

Other features of the book include higher-order discussion questions meant to foster critical thinking and to challenge readers to deeper levels of analysis both on historical and personal/emotional levels so that a deeper/wider perspective of the larger picture of equality could be considered. Also, topics for further study are included to link the reading to other areas of pertinent study. A glossary for each chapter is included.

What is offered is an academic look at some of the more subtle attempts and the lesser-known stories of freedom struggles and civil rights activism. As discussed earlier, a revealing of local activists who parlayed local activities into the dreams of the national movement should become evident. Through their very personal and precious struggles and immense sacrifices, they made differences in the freedom movement. The stories detail the results of the actions of these people and form a perspective of how progress was made over time in an area smaller than the national spectrum but equally if not more important.

ACKNOWLEDGMENTS

I would like to thank Peter Lang Publishing, Inc. for the opportunity to once again share a book worldwide. All of the editors and various people who have been a part of this publication have been marvelously helpful and most gracious as we all worked together through the process. Special thanks to editors Sarah Bode, Shirley Steinberg, Jackie Pavlovic, and Tim Swenarton who guided me through the substantial number of materials necessary for publication and very specially to Dr. Farideh Koohi-Kamali, Senior Vice President of Peter Lang Publishing, Inc. for her initial communications, direct access, and encouragement. Authors are treated with kindly respect and dignity by Peter Lang.

I would also like to thank Marian University for the support it has given me regarding this project. Through the years, Marian has opened the world for me in too many ways to share here. I appreciate that and am thankful for the opportunities. Special thanks to my colleagues in the School of Education, who all have been my mentors either knowingly or not. Clearly, they have helped to inspire any successes I have had. My time with them is exceedingly valuable.

And as always, thanks to my family. Lovely Linda, my wife and best friend for 38 years, has been a constant bright light in my life. She is incredibly uplifting and the strongest person I have ever met. Along with Linda, by far the greatest joy of my life has been raising and knowing our children. I thank Gabe for his steady, strong-willed, and forever advancing spirit about life. He always comes through for everyone. I thank Nancy, cherished daughter-in-law, for her heart of gold and a serious approach to living and loving. And I thank Lucy, the daughter who just never stops, for the way she attacks her life and always goes for the gusto. She can be found almost anywhere doing almost anything. Finally, thanks to Eli, everybody's favorite grandchild, for being the beautiful little guy he is. He helps keep us all connected. By the way these special people lead their lives I can be free to lead mine. I thank them for their independence and my freedom.

INTRODUCTION

Why Are These Stories Important to Tell?

The more we uncover local individuals who risked their lives to repair the past and hope for a better future, the more we see that national civil rights movements gained their success and notoriety on the backs of local heroes. Previously neglected or vastly unfamiliar individuals, both Black and White, who played a part in the history and culture of African Americans deserve to be recognized for their roles in what has evolved through time in the never-ending pursuit of social/civil equality. Local individuals working at local levels formed the basis, the root foundation, of national efforts toward social/civil justice. Without the constant diligence of local individuals which consistently resulted in local movements and local leaders rising up to change a discriminating social/political system, national movements and national leaders might merely share a baseless rhetoric upon which no actions and no results would occur. These local individuals and leaders, whether acting covertly behind the scenes in secret networks or overtly in the streets, schools, and courthouses, made the ultimate difference in whatever progress has been made so far. National leaders and their movements deserve recognition and honor for their broad leadership, which helped to motivate change, and for their courageous and dangerous actions, which surely contributed to the local efforts to end discrimination and create a more equal society. While celebrating the accomplishments of the great and well-known leaders of the broader civil rights movement, this book will focus on the lesser-known but equally important workers for change. An introduction to the text is offered below and the ensuing chapters share more fully the experiences of some of the unheralded men and women unmentioned in historical reports or underplayed in the history of civil rights activism. Their stories need to be told for their own honor and recognition but also as examples of what occurred in cities, towns, and communities throughout the nation. Their locally-driven stories could have happened anywhere for they were unknowingly duplicating the acts of thousands of local men and women far and wide who carried the load of the local movements which supported national leaders.

One of the forgotten African American women unrecognized in history books but of local note in the Midwest is Caroline Quarlls. Ms. Quarlls was the first fugitive slave to travel on the Wisconsin Underground Railroad. Her journey, which began on July 4, 1842, in St. Louis, is described in the chapter entitled *St. Louis to Detroit*. The story begins with a history of the Wisconsin Underground Railroad. The earliest of cities and towns connected to the Underground Railroad such as Platteville, Racine, Milwaukee, and several others are explained as to how they became key stations in the movement of people seeking freedom. The earliest of leaders such as Samuel Smith, C. C. Olin, Dr. Edward Dyer, and more are identified and their ideas are shared. After initial explanation of the Wisconsin Underground Railroad, events, circumstances, and government and citizen actions are described as the story unfolds of the escape of Wisconsin's first fugitive slave. The story is told through the eyes of Quarlls and her conductor, Lyman Goodnow. These two, with the help of over a dozen others, share what it was like on the fugitive slave route to Canada. Close calls, friends, and enemies are all met along the way from St. Louis to Milwaukee back down around Chicago and across Michigan to their final crossing of the Detroit River.

In the milieu of issues leading up to the Civil War, Wisconsin was a microcosm of the controversy surrounding popular sovereignty, states' rights, and the Fugitive Slave Law. A free state, Wisconsin was known for its strong abolition mentality, its Underground Railroad, and its ability to assemble citizens for a cause. When fugitive slave Joshua Glover enters Wisconsin in 1852 and is arrested in 1854, the state rallies to his cause in a fascinating entanglement of federal, state, and local politics and government. The result is the freeing of Glover in what has been called a jailbreak, a rescue, or a release. *Releasing Joshua Glover: Wisconsin's Response to Popular Sovereignty, States' Rights, and the Fugitive Slave Law* begins with an overview of federal and state laws and issues of the period, goes on to describe the Glover arrest and release, and finishes with a review of the aftermath of Glover's disappearance to freedom.

Perhaps the earliest organized attempt to gain freedoms and rights for American women, including African American women, occurred at a conference in Seneca Falls, New York, in 1848. Women and men gathered from a vast range of communities to hold discussion and debate regarding a variety of issues; however, the focus of this conference was voting rights. Women, including Elizabeth Cady Stanton, and men, including Frederick Douglass, wanted to secure women's place in the public forum of voting. Both Elizabeth Cady Stanton and Frederick Douglas, along with a plethora of others, would go on to become icons in the National Association of Women's Clubs movement. This conference seemed to be the beginning in the evolution of colored women's clubs. Throughout the rest of the 1840s and from thence forward local women's clubs originated to participate in a wide range of activities in a variety of areas. Indeed, the right to vote was only one issue in the dozens of personal, social, political, and educational issues this group addressed as it evolved from the Seneca Falls Conference in 1848 to emerge as a national association with clout in 1896. Still active and committed today, the National Association of Colored Women's Clubs has a legacy of triumphs and progress in the liberation of women and, indeed, the personal, social, political, and educational advancement of all African Americans. *The Birth of the National Association of Colored Women's Clubs* describes the background and events which lead to the call by Josephine St. Pierre Ruffin in 1895 for a national meeting of women's clubs to support and connect a national movement for the uplifting of African Americans. Decisions, difficulties, politics, and the relationship to White women's clubs are discussed as well as other related issues. Biographies of key African American leaders such as Mary Church Terrell, Josephine Silone Yates, Lucy Thurman, and Ida B. Wells are reported, and the work these women took on and accomplished is integrated to create a picture of the evolution of progress linked by people and events. The first presidents and the first five years of the national organization are described in detail. Issues and attempts to work on these issues are reported and described. In the end, a remarkable story is told of the fascinating, dedicated, and intelligent accomplishments of African American women that resulted in progress then and progress now to uplift not only African Americans but all Americans.

Uncovering Ezekiel Gillespie: African American Male Suffrage is a description of one person's involvement in gaining African American male voting rights. Though one of many key players in eventually passing state law for Black male suffrage, Ezekiel Gillespie is widely unknown in the nation and even in Wisconsin, the state in which he made his mark on history. This story explains who Gillespie was, what his contributions were, and what resulted from his contributions. Along the way, it describes what primarily is known of his personal and political life, his involvement in equal rights causes, and the people he associated with who helped him establish a permanent effect in favor of African American voting rights. The story also attempts to offer perspectives on Gillespie's motives, which can be used to foster further discussion and investigation of his life and his works. Most importantly, the story chronicles Ezekiel Gillespie's prominent role in the unusual circumstances that led to the passing of voting rights for African American males. The court case of *Gillespie v. Palmer* serves as the most tangible evidence supporting uncovering Ezekiel Gillespie as an important contributor to the history of African Americans. Both the case and Gillespie himself are essential to preserve.

The struggle for fair and open housing in Milwaukee reached its climax in 1967. *Milwaukee Movers: James Groppi/Vel Phillips* explores the African American population growth historically in the city of Milwaukee and how this population came to be segregated in terms of housing. Discussion includes the perceptions, policies, and actions of the mayor, police chief, and the Milwaukee Common Council during the crucial 1960s. Because schools mirror society, the events described in this chapter link to the unequal treatment of education and the politics of racism. The chapter provides a segue to the next chapter which has education as its focus. Further, the story develops the evolution of change that occurred over time, specifically 1963–1968, which eventuated in laws impacting the concept of fair and open housing. Key leaders, particularly James Groppi and Vel Phillips, are discussed as local icons within the Black community in the establishment of open housing laws.

Lloyd Barbee was an inspirational leader at a time when inspiration was needed to move the Milwaukee Public Schools away from segregation and into a new era of equality and human rights. *Attorney for the Plaintiffs: Desegregating Milwaukee Public Schools* describes the give-and-take battles that resulted when Lloyd Barbee took on the leadership of challenging the existing entrenched and racist segregated system of schools in order to desegregate and provide educational, civic, and human rights for children and adults. A person of integrity and action, Lloyd Barbee rose through the ranks of local and state chapters of the National Association for the Advancement of Colored People (NAACP) as well as forming and leading a substantial number of social activist groups. Considered both a cultured man and an intellectual, Barbee spent time both in the halls of justice and on the street. He spoke truth to power in formal settings and walked his talk on the pavement. His work inspired the citizens of Milwaukee to stand up and fight for a change in the system. A dedicated and shrewd lawyer, Barbee was lead attorney for the court case named *Amos et al. v. Board of School Directors of the City of Milwaukee*. This monumental court battle pitting the status quo against the purveyors of change regarding desegregation in Milwaukee Public Schools dominated Barbee's life and ended in controversy. An iconic court case by an iconic local figure in Lloyd Barbee, this lawsuit defines the struggle for desegregation in Milwaukee and across the nation.

This book consists of a series of chapters regarding real people who are not so well known in the mainstream of American freedom and civil rights discussions. These people have made a difference by the events of their lives and by the deliberate contributions they made in the evolution of American freedom and civil rights. In one chapter, depictions of fugitive slaves create awareness of the perils of freedom runs and of the desperate, dangerous, and terrifying life of being a hunted person. This awareness, accompanied by the new knowledge of those who helped forge a path to freedom, moved America closer to dismantling racist discrimination. Other chapters reveal the degree of local level blockage Black individuals needed to struggle through to gain measures of civil rights and the determination and staying power these people had to have to navigate the system and to advance progress toward a more just society. Still other chapters point out major local efforts by diligent, but for the most part unknown, local people that result in court case settlements and state laws to advance civil rights. These, in turn, helped to create a better awareness by the masses regarding the inequality that existed and the oppression that it caused. In particular, voting rights, housing rights, and school desegregation battles on local and state levels are described and analyzed. Finally, one chapter takes a close look at Black involvement in women's clubs and how Black leaders, both local and national, defined women's roles in the Black freedom and civil rights movements and how those leaders forged a path toward the acceptance of Black women into White women's clubs to form integrated clubs working toward common goals. Themes of the chapters stand out as they all build upon each other and are seen from one chapter to the next. In the end, a subtle evolution of ideas can be realized that forms the notion that the great and recognized Black leaders in history have their important place but that freedom and civil rights advancements are made on the backs of the local unknowns who need to be recognized for what they have contributed. This uncovering of unknown players involved in crucial events of their times in the quest for social, political, civil, and personal equality and freedom provides a unique perspective somewhat counter to mainstream thinking. These stories need to be told to uncover the people and the issues in historical perspective regarding the slow, grinding, difficult evolution of efforts meant to gain some foothold in the quest for equality. Local efforts leading to national movements set the stage for changes in thinking regarding social/civil rights and equality and made possible the movement toward a more equal society.

· 1 ·

ST. LOUIS TO DETROIT

"May a slave look at a liberty pole?"
—Caroline Quarlls, 1842

By design, the Wisconsin Underground Railroad was quite a secretive operation. The necessity of keeping silent about protecting and moving fugitive slaves created not only success in saving people from slavery but also failure at recording much of the history of the operation. From personal stories and a few well-publicized episodes, a knowledge that the Wisconsin Underground Railroad existed and succeeded can be derived, but deep details and multiple cases are by and large absent. Nevertheless, it is estimated that more than 100 fugitive slaves successfully found their way to Canada and other areas via the help of the Wisconsin residents involved in the Underground Railroad in the years 1842–1861 (Wisconsin Historical Society, n.d.).

Before the term *abolitionist* became popular in the 1800s, there were efforts on the parts of certain groups to help slaves escape their masters and run to freedom far away from Southern plantations and harsh masters. These efforts were often begun by individuals acting out of religious beliefs but evolved into organized efforts by like-minded church groups and community members. These individuals and groups started their work as early as the colonial period and were forerunners to the turbulent and volatile attention given to the concept of slavery as the 1800s began and moved toward the Civil War. As the years from 1800 to 1860 unfolded, abolition groups became more and more active in assisting fugitive slaves to freedom. Paths, trails, and stationhouses became organized routes to freedom. These organized routes became known as the Underground Railroad.

The term *Underground Railroad* was probably used for these endeavors because of the newness and popularity of steam locomotives and railways beginning in the 1820s. It was more a metaphor than a reality for most fugitive slaves avoided the use of the railway in their escapes to freedom. In fact, they avoided any situation that would bring notice to them. In addition, there is a popular belief that the term *underground* was used because there was a system of underground tunnels built in which fugitive slaves would travel to their northern destinations. Contrary to popular belief, though there were tunnels built here and there mostly between buildings, there was no regional or national organization of tunnels. There were, however, in many cases, highly organized groups of people who would pass off fugitives from one to another on the way to free states, Canada, or even other countries. These people and groups were called the *conductors* of the Underground Railroad. The peak years of abolitionist efforts in the Wisconsin Underground Railroad with its 100-plus cases of escapes were reached from 1830 to 1865. On a national level, it is reported that as many as 100,000 enslaved persons may have escaped via various Underground Railroads in the years between the American Revolution and the Civil War (Murrell, 2004).

While celebrating the works of known abolitionists and others who dedicated their lives to guiding fugitive slaves to freedom, it is also important to realize that the majority of assistance to fugitive slaves came from other involved Blacks and also from Blacks in nonslave states. Especially before 1830, the largest assistance for shelter, financial support, and geographic route direction came from organized efforts of Northern free Blacks (Murrell, 2004). This is not to diminish the work of White people prior to or after 1830; rather, it is to present an accurate account of the beginnings of the Wisconsin Underground Railroad as early enslaved Blacks, and especially Northern free Blacks, worked out complicated systems of communication and escape route logistics. After 1830, more Whites began to publicly support abolition, thus increasing the number of Whites who became involved in assisting fugitive slaves. There continued to be, however, large numbers of Blacks both in leadership and support positions of the Underground Railroad. In addition, personal diaries and letters point out that not only did people of different races work together toward assisting fugitive slaves after 1830, people of different races *and* genders worked together. In this way, ending slavery, or at least escaping slavery, opened doors to other aspects of dealing with differences. In the end, the essence of Underground Railroads should not be measured only in terms of the number of attempted or successful escapes from slavery, but in the idea that it exposed slavery for what it was, resisted it as a concept, and perhaps brought races and genders together in a common cause. In addition, because Blacks were the early organizers and remained key leaders, the Wisconsin Underground Railroad helped to refute the myth that African Americans could not act or organize on their own.

The Wisconsin Territory, established in 1836, was formed under the Northwest Ordinance of 1787. The same Northwest Ordinance guided Wisconsin to statehood in 1848. This is important to note because under the Northwest Ordinance of 1787 slavery was forbidden in Wisconsin. Therefore, very early in Wisconsin history a trend and mindset of antislavery was established. This followed through as Wisconsin remained an abolitionist hotbed throughout the 1800s. In spite of this, masters brought their slaves to Wisconsin to work in the lead mining industry of the southwestern areas of Wisconsin near Platteville. Having made the journey north, upon their arrival in Wisconsin masters were often surprised to have their slaves freed by area community members and local authorities. This was in keeping with the established law. Almost by accident, some slaves suddenly found themselves free. These freed slaves often became workers on the Wisconsin Underground Railroad. Other African Americans, however, continued to work in the mines as slaves due to various delays, perhaps bribes, and other procedures taken by masters to avoid losing them. To counter this, following the ideas of immigrant leaders near Platteville such as James Bennet McCord and Alvin McCord Dixen, citizens organized an abolitionist movement against the slave masters to force the freedom of slaves who were still controlled by masters in Wisconsin. The success of these immigrant leaders caused Platteville to be dubbed "Abolition Hollow" (Murrell, 2004).

The southeastern part of Wisconsin, especially Racine, was also strongly abolitionist. It was in Racine County in 1840 that Wisconsin's first abolition society was formed. This society and Racine County in general played an important role in Wisconsin's first fugitive slave escape to freedom, its most well-known escape to freedom, and countless other sketchy and unreported escapes to freedom. Newspapers played a large role in abolitionist efforts by publishing strongly stated antislavery editorials and by reporting any news regarding antislavery issues. Two notable newspapers in the 1840s were the *Aegis*, published in Racine, and the *Free Democrat*, published in Milwaukee. These two newspapers, along with others such as the *Waukesha Freeman*, fueled the debate over slavery and abolition.

Churches have also long been associated with the abolitionist viewpoint. In Beloit, another southeastern Wisconsin town, Presbyterian and Congregational church members resolved that:

> In view of this convention American slavery is a sin; that it is a sin of such magnitude that all who practice it or knowingly promote it should be excluded from our pulpits and the fellowship of our churches; that while we deprecate all harsh language and rash measures in the destruction of this evil, we will nevertheless avail ourselves of all suitable measures to enlighten and correct the public mind in regard to the sin of slavery. (Wisconsin Historical Society, n.d., p. 1)

In addition to these two religions, Quakers also had a long history of participating in the Underground Railroad, and Quaker houses were always open to assist fugitive slaves. This is indicative of people in Wisconsin bonding together in proabolitionist thinking and action. These groups and like-minded individuals did much to establish and organize the Wisconsin Underground Railroad.

At the same time as these first decades of Wisconsin state history, the plantations of the Southern states were flourishing. Their cotton crops were extremely abundant and workers were sorely needed. This boom for plantation owners caused an increase in the value of slaves. Slaves, however, continued to seek their freedom in escape from harsh masters to Northern states. Michigan, Pennsylvania, Ohio, Indiana, Illinois, and Wisconsin became regular destinations. From the South, northward routes were mapped out and fugitive slave stations were established. Abolitionists organized networks of trusted friends to fugitive slaves so that safe travel could be led by conductors of the Underground Railroad. Chicago became a standard hub city to the usual target final destination of Canada (Putnam, 1907). Because slaves were increasing in value to the plantation owners, the plantation owners increased their efforts to keep their slaves. And when slaves ran away, plantation owners increased their efforts to get them back. As a result, slave owners would hire bounty hunters, often called slave catchers, to find their runaway slaves and bring them back. Great efforts were put into the retrieval of runaway slaves. Some plantation owners even went after the slaves themselves.

As the Wisconsin Underground Railroad developed, slave catchers found that retrieving slaves became more and more difficult because of the distances slaves were able to run and the sophistication and organization of the escape routes. By 1850, with a majority of Congress still proslavery, heavy emphasis was put on the issue of slave loss. This resulted in the passage of the Fugitive Slave Law of 1850 (Putnam, 1907). This powerful law, slanted totally in favor of the plantation owners and against fugitive slaves, gave leeway to plantation owners to seek and find runaway slaves. They were even allowed to appeal to local authorities to help catch the runaways in order to return them to the plantations. The law also made it illegal for anyone to go against the return of slaves by assisting in their escapes. In fact, the law made it illegal to even withhold information without providing help. The law forced all citizens to help return all escaping slaves to plantation owners. Anyone who refused to assist authorities, or who helped slaves in any way, was subject to heavy penalties (Wisconsin Historical Society, n.d.). The Fugitive Slave Law of 1850 created even more antislavery feelings among citizens of Wisconsin. Both Wisconsin legislative houses voted against the passage of this law and political conventions in Waterford, Milwaukee, and Waukesha condemned the law. The Fugitive Slave Law of 1850 became a rallying point for abolitionists who felt morally compelled to disobey it and so became criminals in the eyes of the law (Wisconsin Historical Society, n.d.).

In addition to Platteville, Racine, Beloit, and Milwaukee, proabolition centers of activity developed all over the state in such places as Waukesha, Waupun, Ripon, Spring Prairie, Milton, and Fond du Lac. In addition to McCord and Dixen, some three dozen or more other people are identified as Wisconsin antislavery leaders. In addition to Abolition Hollow, there were particular places well established as major elements in the Wisconsin Underground Railroad. Two such particular places were the Milton House in Milton (National Park Service, n.d.) and the Willard Pond Farm in Alto Township (Fairwater Historical Society, 2000). Both of these served often as safe houses on the road to freedom in the Wisconsin Underground Railroad. By 1840, the Wisconsin Underground Railroad was an established institution (Putnam, 1907).

Although stories exist of fugitive slaves passing through Wisconsin from 1839 to 1842, the first fugitive slave identified by name to move through an organized Wisconsin Underground Railroad was Caroline Quarlls (Quarrels, Quarles, Quarrelles, Quarlis). Reports of her story vary considerably in regard to her name, specific dates of travel, and details of her escape. Some recollections age her at 15 when she arrived in Wisconsin, some state she was 16, some state she was 18, and still others report she was somewhere between 13 and 15. Two well-known abolitionists among the many who helped Quarlls, C. C. Olin, editor of the *Waukesha Freeman*, and Lyman Goodnow, a farmer, remember her as either 15 or 16 years old. Both of these gentlemen support 1842 as the time of arrival in Wisconsin for Quarlls. Other reports indicate it was 1843 when she came to Wisconsin. All reports considered, it appears that fugitive Caroline Quarlls was a 16-year-old Black slave from St. Louis who left her master on July 4, 1842, and traveled by steamboat to Alton, Illinois, and then by stagecoach to Milwaukee where she arrived during the first week of August in 1842.

Quarlls was a slave of wealthy St. Louis merchant Charles R. Hall. She had learned to become an excellent seamstress and an especially good embroiderer. She provided these skills for Mrs. Hall while also acting as her personal servant. For some unreported reason, Mrs. Hall became angry with Quarlls one day and cut off her hair, which was reported to be long and beautiful (Siebert, n.d.). This event triggered the efforts by Quarlls to leave. She had been thinking of doing so for a time despite not despising her mistress and acknowledging that she could possibly be related to her. In her later years, Quarlls stated that enslavement for her wasn't as harsh as it was for others; yet, she resisted being owned. She was fortunate enough to have a free woman as a grandmother who might have given her $100 to set her on her way (Dwinnell, 1867). Maintaining her composure and planning her escape, Quarlls obtained permission from Hall to visit a sick friend. Before leaving for the visit, Quarlls bundled some clothes and personal items and threw them out her bedroom window. She went to visit the sick friend and afterward stopped to pick up her bundle. Then, pretending to be a White girl going off to school, she tricked the steamboat clerk at the local dock and boarded a steamboat to Alton, Illinois.

Quarlls was light skinned and had a long straight nose and thin lips. One memoir, written by Soloman Ashley Dwinnell, claims that she was part Indian based on her great-grandmother's ancestry. Thinking she was only part African American, Dwinnell called her an octoroon (Dwinnell, 1867). Because of her light skin and facial features, she thought she could join White girls in Alton and attend a White school with them without being noticed as a Black girl and a fugitive slave. However, a Black man saw through this plan. Knowing she was a Black girl, he told her she would be found out as a Black and a slave. This man sent Quarlls on to Milwaukee where she went to a station called the Milwaukee House. By this time, Mrs. Hall had indeed sent slave catchers to get Quarlls, but Quarlls was not aware of it yet.

At the Milwaukee House, another Black man offered to hide her at his place. This man was a barber by the name of Titball (Titbull) who volunteered to the Milwaukee House but apparently had not proven his trust. Titball befriended Quarlls and after a week's time she did trust and have confidence in him, even trusting him with $40 of her money. However, in the second week when Mrs. Hall's slave catchers came around, Titball sold Quarlls out for $100. Titball led the slave catchers to his house where Quarlls was hiding. Fortunately for Quarlls, the network apparently had built-in safeguards to watch unproven volunteers. A Black boy got wind of the sellout and was able to alert Quarlls and move her to another location before the slave catchers arrived with Titball. Titball lost his $100 (Goodnow, n.d.).

The slave catchers, however, plowed on and didn't stop their search for Quarlls. Indeed, their efforts intensified because they thought they were closing in on her. They began searching streets and houses all around Titball's house. But as was the case during the entire Quarlls episode and all the other fugitive escapes, abolitionists kept low profiles, kept out of sight, feigned a lack of interest in fugitives and a focused interest on daily life, and, above all, caused no stir. While abolitionists stayed invisible, the proslavery population was very visible and caused quite a stir whenever the rumor of a fugitive about was heard. A Milwaukee attorney named Asahel Finch quietly took Quarlls to the Milwaukee River and got her across where she hid all day under a hogshead (Siebert, n.d.). That night she was taken to a farm out of the city owned by a person, Samuel Brown, reported to be the first conductor on the Wisconsin Underground Railroad (Dwinnell, 1867). Brown then took her the next day to Father Samuel Dougherty's (Daugherty) house in Pewaukee. As they traveled to Dougherty's house, the slave catchers, named Spencer and Arnold, and a posse-like group passed the wagon in which Quarlls hid (Siebert, n.d.). Knowing the slave catchers were close behind, another abolitionist named Ezra Mendell took her to Waukesha (then called Prairieville) to stay at the home of Deacon Allen Clinton. When Mendell returned home, the slave catchers were at his house demanding to search it. With the assistance of a rifle, he refused the search. Hearing reports of a reward for Quarlls and a continued and accelerated searching by the slave catchers, Mendell and abolitionist Lyman Goodnow later took Quarlls another 30 miles to the home of Solomon Dwinnell near Spring Prairie and left her there. Returning to Spring Prairie sometime later, Goodnow, a 43-year-old bachelor with no children, was chosen as conductor of the final 500 miles via the Wisconsin Underground Railroad to Canada. This successful journey took three weeks to accomplish. And as in the case of most fugitive slaves, many would help along the way.

It was early September of 1842 when Goodnow agreed to conduct Caroline Quarlls around Chicago across Indiana and Michigan and to Detroit, where the plan was to have her cross to Canada. When Goodnow returned to Dwinnell's place to pick Quarlls up, she had been moved again to a Mr. Peffer's house. Arriving at her new hiding place, Goodnow and several abolitionists were devising a plan of travel when Dr. Edward Galusha Dyer of Burlington arrived. Dyer was a devoted antislavery activist. He was called a *double abolitionist*, a term used for people who spoke out against slavery, helped people run away, *and* gave money for the cause. According to Goodnow's personal memoirs, Dyer proved to be a "commander-in-chief, strong abolitionist, and best friend to humanity" (Dwinnell, 1867, para. XXXII). While a good horse and buggy was gotten for Goodnow, Dyer went home and collected food and money for the trip. When he came back, Dyer passed the hat among the abolitionists and collected $12. Goodnow added this to the five dollars he had gotten from Clinton and the three dollars he had himself to total $20. Dr. Dyer had also written a glowing letter of appeal for help from all abolitionists and all those willing to help a human being to freedom. Goodnow reported that Dyer's letter would "move a heart of stone" (Goodnow, n.d. p. 6). With the $20, the letter, most likely a list of trusted friends of the Wisconsin Underground Railroad, and a pillowcase full of food, Goodnow and Quarlls left Burlington.

A detailed summary of the precarious but successful trip on the Wisconsin Underground Railroad would include too many events and details to report in this writing; however, a general account based on the writings of Lyman Goodnow of the passage of Wisconsin's first identified fugitive slave, Caroline Quarlls of St. Louis, Missouri, follows (Goodnow, n.d.).

On the first day out, after enduring a pouring rain with Quarlls hidden under a buffalo robe on the floor of the buggy, Goodnow and Quarlls stopped for refuge at the house of a Methodist minister named Russell. Russell was not an outspoken abolitionist, but as was the case with many clergy, he was antislavery and willing to help a human being to freedom. He provided food, shelter, and protection for Quarlls and Goodnow. Goodnow was impressed enough with Russell to make him a stationmaster on the Wisconsin Underground Railroad. This is part of how the Wisconsin Underground Railroad recruited its trusted friends, conductors, and, in this case, stationmasters. Russell's house became a station on the Wisconsin Underground Railroad. Goodnow was creating networks as he went.

On the second day out, one of the stops was at a Deacon Fowler's house. At Fowler's house, there were several young girls about the same age as Quarlls. The Fowler girls provided clothing for Quarlls, which included a dress, some gloves, a thick veil, and a small reticule. Quarlls used the thick veil to conceal her face, and she put the few jewels she had in the reticule. After a brief visit, Goodnow and Quarlls were on the road again.

On the fourth day out, they arrived at a Mr. Beebe's house. Mr. Beebe had just returned from Chicago where he had seen a reward poster for $300 for Quarlls. Beebe also found out that in addition to Spencer and Arnold, the clerk of the steamboat on which Quarlls traveled to Alton, Illinois, was now visiting all the lake ports looking for her and advertising for her. In the usual proslavery manner, he was creating quite a stir getting people excited about finding a fugitive. The steamboat company was obligated to pay Mrs. Hall $800 if Quarlls wasn't found, and the steamboat company was holding the clerk who let her on board accountable. He in turn was making a big effort to capture the girl who tricked him. In the end, because of the successful escape by Goodnow and Quarlls, this $800 was paid to Mrs. Hall by the steamboat company. No record exists of what happened to the clerk.

In later years, Goodnow told the story of leaving Beebe's house and stopping at a church. Sunday school teachers wanted to meet and speak to Caroline. They asked many questions. Quarlls answered the questions directly and then asked one herself that caught the teachers off guard. During the conversation, Quarlls noticed a liberty pole nearby. She asked the teachers what it was for. The teachers answered that it was to commemorate the birth of liberty in America. Quarlls then asked what they did with the liberty pole and the teachers replied that they looked at it (and probably sometimes danced around it). When she heard this answer, Quarlls asked if a slave may look at a liberty pole. Silence fell onto the group. The teachers could not answer Caroline's question. The pastor tried but he could not answer either. Goodnow was startled and impressed that Quarlls was only 16 and could not read nor write but had befuddled the teachers. Goodnow clearly admired and respected Caroline's ability as he took delight in telling this story (Goodnow, n.d.).

On another night, Goodnow and Quarlls befriended a German man and his wife who lived in a bare shanty and had very little means. Nevertheless, the Germans, who apparently assumed Quarlls was a White girl, put the two travelers up for a night and gave them what they could to eat. Goodnow later reported that he had been advised by leaders in the Wisconsin Underground Railroad to trust Germans because the German immigrants had a proven record of loyalty. Goodnow went to great lengths in stating that he never met a German who was not antislavery except "those who were Yankeefied" (Goodnow, n.d., para. XXXVI).

For several days of the journey Goodnow and Quarlls traveled among Quaker homes, villages, and regions. This must have been an especially safe feeling for the two who were used to being on edge and on the lookout constantly. The Quakers through their trusted cooperation and help provided as much as a safe haven as possible on this leg of the Underground Railroad. It happened that at this time all the Quaker men were away at a convention in Ohio. The women Quakers, it was reported, would say nothing about an escape route but would always tell where the next Quaker house was at a convenient location (Siebert, n.d.). In other words, it seemed they didn't outwardly recognize the Underground Railroad nor did they generally speak out about members of it. Nevertheless, they did know about it, they did take part in it, and they were members of it.

After taking a wide swing around Chicago and going north to avoid being noticed by the many people in the area, Goodnow and Quarlls now cut a straight path across Michigan toward Detroit. Near a town called Climax Prairie Goodnow arranged for a Black man to put the pair up for a night. He reported that this man was harsh and unfriendly and did not treat them right. For these reasons, they probably did not trust this man, spent a restless night with worry of being found out, and were anxious to leave the next morning. In the morning, as they left in a hurry, Quarlls forgot her reticule, which contained her jewelry and some remaining money. When they realized their loss, they had traveled too far to go back. The jewels were all Quarlls had left to remember her home.

Reaching Ann Arbor, they stayed with Guy Beckley, the editor of the newspaper *Signal of Liberty*, a heavily abolitionist newspaper. After a good night's rest in a trusted environment, they set out for Detroit. Surprisingly, they met up along the way with a group of 32 fugitive slaves near Battle Creek who were traveling the Underground Railroad to freedom. They also had relied heavily on Quaker assistance, and these fugitives feared no danger as they headed for Canada. This group had the luxury of three veteran conductors who acted as an advanced team several miles ahead of the group. They scouted out slave catchers and safe stations. After a brief time with this group, Goodnow and Quarlls set out on their own again. Another experience occurred shortly after they left the

32 fugitives. Just before Detroit, Goodnow and Quarlls met a former slave and her husband from St. Louis who were also heading to Canada. Oddly enough, Quarlls and the woman had known each other in St. Louis.

At about 6:00 p.m. on a Tuesday night, Goodnow and Quarlls reached Detroit. As the streets were filled with workers returning home at the end of a day's work, Goodnow quickly sought out the last station before Canada. This was Ambler's Station, which was located on the banks of the Detroit River. Mr. Ambler was not at home but Mrs. Ambler received them well. Before leaving on business, Mr. Ambler had assigned two men to stand by to help ferry the fugitive across the river to freedom in Sandwich, Ontario (now Windsor). Mrs. Ambler sent for the two men. It had been three weeks since Goodnow and Quarlls had begun their journey. They were now near the end. Goodnow paid out the first money he had spent on the trip: two dollars to the two men to ferry both himself and Quarlls across the river. It seemed the general call to friends of abolitionists had paid off for now they were crossing the river to Caroline's freedom. Not only did the two make it to Canada and freedom for Quarlls, but, with the exception of the one station at Climax Prairie, they were treated with care all along the way with well-planned routes, shelter, food, clothing, and protection from dozens of friends and workers on the Underground Railroad.

When the boat crossed the river and met the banks of Canada, Quarlls experienced a flood of emotions including disbelief. She became overcome with grief and crying and doubted that she was in Canada. Possibly out of relief over the journey's end, she felt insecure with the reality of the situation and begged Goodnow to convince her that Sandwich was not St. Louis. In her exuberance and relief, she imagined she had been tricked into ending up right back in St. Louis. Everything looked like St. Louis to Quarlls. It took some time, but Goodnow finally convinced her that she was in Canada (Goodnow, n.d.). When he was certain that she was all right, Goodnow took her to the home of a Reverend Haskell. Goodnow then recrossed the Detroit River and headed for home. As he began his journey from Detroit back to home, he found that the steamboat clerk had been at the Detroit River for two weeks watching every ferryboat that crossed the river. This final near-capture is testimony to the constant danger fugitive slaves faced in their journeys to freedom. It is also testimony to the intelligence and bravery with which the members of the Wisconsin Underground Railroad carried out their mission to establish liberty and freedom for enslaved human beings.

On the way home, Goodnow stopped back at the place in Climax Prairie where Quarlls and he had left in a hurry and Quarlls had left her reticule.

Goodnow stopped to retrieve Caroline's reticule, which held her jewels and money. The man who had previously treated them harshly now refused to give the items back to Goodnow. After some arguing, Goodnow realized the man was not going to give up the items so he must have struck a deal with him. If Goodnow got a letter from a local abolitionist, Dr. Thayer, asking for the items back, the man would agree to give them up. Apparently, the man doubted Goodnow could obtain such a letter and thought he would be rid of Goodnow. However, if so, he underestimated Lyman Goodnow. His horse tired from such a long journey, Goodnow walked the five miles to Dr. Thayer's house, waited over a day for Thayer to return home, obtained an angry letter from Thayer ordering the man to give up the items, and trudged back to the man's house. At this point the man gave up Caroline's possessions, and Goodnow headed back to Milwaukee. He stopped briefly at Father Dougherty's house in Pewaukee to pick up a few more things Quarlls had left there because she was unable to take them with her. Upon arriving at his home again, Goodnow packaged Caroline's possessions and sent them to her at Haskell's via a Dr. Porter in Detroit who confirmed that she had received them (Goodnow, n.d.).

Goodnow then went back to the Milwaukee barber who sold Quarlls out to the slave catchers for the $100. Though Titball did not receive the $100 from the slave catchers because Quarlls had gotten away, he did have the $40 that Quarlls had given him for safekeeping after she had begun to trust him. Goodnow asked Titball to give the $40 back so he could send it to Quarlls. Titball claimed that he never had $40 from Quarlls and refused to give Goodnow any money. Goodnow went to court and sued. He won the suit but Titball died before Goodnow got the $40 back (Dwinnell, 1867).

In April of 1880, some 38 years after their joining the Wisconsin Underground Railroad, Goodnow received a letter from Caroline Quarlls. He had received others as well. Goodnow learned that Caroline took up schooling in her first year in Canada and had learned to read and write. In 1845, she had married an older man by the name of Allen Watkins. Using the Wisconsin Underground Railroad, Watkins escaped through Wisconsin across Michigan and into Canada where he met and married Quarlls. He found work on a farm as a cook. It was believed to be the same farm at which Quarlls worked, and perhaps that is where they met. Through these letters, Goodnow learned about the unfolding of key events in Caroline's life. He learned of her unhappiness over the deaths of her mother, her sister, and Mrs. Hall. He learned that Caroline had had six children, three boys and three girls, and that she had made sure that they all were educated for employment. Quarlls told him that Reverend Haskell was not the person Goodnow thought he was and that he was a dark-sided man. She didn't explain any details, but it was clear she intended something serious. Quarlls was passionate about her experiences with Goodnow and the Underground Railroad. After telling him that she was still alive, working hard, and living in the same place where he had left her, she told him that she had never forgotten him or his kindness. She stated that she would like to see him one more time before she died to return thanks for his kindness toward her (Goodnow, n.d.).

It is not known if the two ever saw each other again. It is doubtful and no record exists. What is known is that Caroline Quarlls, said to be Wisconsin's first fugitive slave, and her conductor Lyman Goodnow, said to have made the longest and most difficult run of any conductor, established a popular route on the Wisconsin Underground Railroad. Many of the 100 fugitive slaves who successfully journeyed the Wisconsin Underground Railroad to Canada and many more unreported fugitive slaves traveled the routes that Goodnow and Quarlis carved out to arrive safely in a land of liberty—Canada via the Wisconsin Underground Railroad.

Glossary

Abolitionists: People who favor the abolition of slavery.
Abolition Hollow: The nickname for Platteville, Wisconsin, because of its success at freeing slaves.
Aegis: A nineteenth century newspaper in Racine County, Wisconsin, that was well known for its abolitionist viewpoints.
Alton, Illinois: A city in the free state of Illinois on the Mississippi River about fifteen miles north of St. Louis.
Conductors: People who acted as trail guides and helpers in the freedom runs of fugitive slaves on the Underground Railroad.
Double Abolitionists: People who spoke out against slavery, helped out in freedom runs, *and* contributed money for the cause.
Freed Slaves: A former slave who has been released from slavery by legal means either by manumission or by emancipation.
Free Democrat: A nineteenth century Milwaukee, Wisconsin, newspaper that was well known for its abolitionist viewpoints and its activism for civil rights.
Free States: States in which slavery was illegal.
Fugitive Slaves: Servants or slaves who were on the run from their owners/masters.
Liberty Pole: A tall wooden pole ornamented in the name of liberty planted in the ground usually in town squares.

Northwest Ordinance of 1787: A law passed in 1787 to regulate the settlement of the Northwest Territory.

Quakers: A Christian movement founded in 1650 by George Fox devoted to peaceful life principles that were guided by a personal "inner light."

Sandwich, Ontario: A Canadian city just across the Detroit River from Detroit, Michigan, which was renamed Windsor in 1935.

Signal of Liberty: An antislavery newspaper established in 1833 in Ann Arbor, Michigan.

Slave States: States in which slavery was legal.

Reticule: A woman's drawstring handbag.

Underground Railroad: The network of people who worked toward freeing slaves by helping them to escape to a land of freedom.

Waukesha Freeman: A nineteenth century Waukesha, Wisconsin, newspaper which featured news and stories regarding fugitive slaves and other civil rights issues.

Discussion/Reflection

1. What is your analysis of Caroline's decision to leave Mrs. Hall and St. Louis? Do you think she made the right decision? Why or why not?
2. What would you have done if you had been the one attacked by Mrs. Hall? What should Caroline have done?
3. If Caroline was unhappy living in Canada, why didn't she return to the United States?
4. How would you describe the relationship between Caroline and Lyman Goodnow? Be sure to cite details from the chapter that support your description.
5. What does this story tell you about how you feel about social injustice? Why?
6. Why do you think Caroline and Goodnow never saw each other again after the crossing to Canada?
7. Look up the song *Follow the Drinking Gourd* and see what it means. What special significance does it have for slaves on the road to freedom? Then listen to the song.
8. Choose one of the song titles below and investigate and explain the significance of the song to African Americans. Then listen to the song.

    a. *Swing Low, Sweet Chariot*
    b. *Wade in the Water*
    c. *The Gospel Train*

9. Using information from the chapter, chart a path on a map showing the journey Caroline took to freedom.
10. Imagine Caroline on the deck of the steamship from St. Louis to Alton. How do you think she dressed? How do you think she acted? What activities do you think she undertook?

Selected Topics for Further Study

1. Underground Railroad
2. Issues that resulted in the American Civil War
3. American slavery
4. Northwest Ordinance of 1787
5. Your local history regarding ethnic populations
6. African American newspapers
7. Quakers and Methodists
8. Southern plantations
9. Fugitive Slave Law of 1850
10. Fugitive slave memoirs and letters
11. Abolitionists memoirs and letters
12. Alton, Illinois
13. Liberty poles
14. Immigrant status in the nineteenth century
15. Detroit, Michigan
16. Detroit River
17. Windsor, Ontario
18. Gospel songs on the Underground Railroad
19. African American leaders in freedom seeking
20. Nineteenth century laws impacting ethnic minorities

References

Dwinnell, S. A. (1867). Wisconsin as it was and as it is 1836 compared with 1866: Its material, educational and religious history. Wisconsin Historical Society. Retrieved from athttp://www.wisconsinhistory.org/turningpoints/search.asp?id=1558

Fairwater Historical Society (2000). National Park Service visits Pond Farm near Fairwater. Retrieved from www.wlhn.org/fairwater_histsoc/Early%20Newsletters/newsletter_jun00/newsletter_jun00.htm

Goodnow, L. (n.d.). Lyman Goodnow, Recollection, 1880? [Unpublished Transcription]. State of Wisconsin Collection, University of Wisconsin, Madison, WI. Retrieved from http://digital.library.wisc.edu/1711.dl/WI.Goodnow2e

Murrell, J. (2004). Underground Railroad ran through Wisconsin. *The Madison Times*. Retrieved from http://www.madtimes.com/archives/feb2004_3/top_story1.htm

National Park Service (n.d.). Aboard the Underground Railroad. Retrieved from https://www.nps.gov/nr/travel/underground/wi1.htm

Putnam, Dora (1907). The Underground Railway in Wisconsin. *Waukesha Freeman*. Retrieved from http://www.wisconsinhistory.org/turningpoints/search.asp?id=1560

Siebert, W. H. (n.d.). C. C. Olin's account of Caroline Quarrells. *The Underground Railroad of Wisconsin Network to Freedom*. Retrieved from http://www.genealogy.mylinktothepast.com/p16952.htm

Wisconsin Historical Society. (n.d.). The Underground Railroad in Wisconsin. Retrieved from http://www.wisconsinhistory.org/Content.aspx?dsNav=N:4294963828-4294963805&dsRecordDetailS=R:CS566

· 2 ·

RELEASING JOSHUA GLOVER

Wisconsin's Response to Popular Sovereignty, States' Rights, and the Fugitive Slave Law

"A man's liberty is at stake!"
—Sherman Booth on March 11, 1854

Black people had been living in what is now the state of Wisconsin since the eighteenth century. French fur traders had brought Blacks with them as slaves in the 1700s (Baker, 2006, p. 63). By the early nineteenth century, there were both Black slaves in Wisconsin and a number of free Blacks (Murrell, 2004). After 1848, when Wisconsin became a state, free Blacks were living throughout the state and most especially in the southern and southeastern portions of Wisconsin. It was typical that Blacks either lived among each other in agricultural communes in rural areas or in networks and neighborhoods in urban areas. Both provided security, protection, and support for Black people. Cities were found to be more advantageous for Blacks because of more employment opportunities and an easier time creating networks. By 1850, Milwaukee County had the second largest population of Blacks in Wisconsin. In the 1850 census, 111 Blacks registered and 98 of those lived in the city of Milwaukee, which had 19,963 as a total population. Unlike its southern neighbor, Racine, Milwaukee was not known for its proabolitionist thinking (Pferdehirt, 1998). In fact, slave owners frequently used Milwaukee lawyers to assist them in the rendition of fugitives. Racine County, unlike Milwaukee County, was a hotbed of antislavery/abolitionist thinking. Leaders in the abolition movement congregated in several areas of this southeastern portion of the state. These leaders working in and around the city of Racine played a large role in the controversy over free and enslaved Blacks.

As stated in Chapter 1, at the same time as these first decades of Wisconsin state history, the plantations of the Southern states were flourishing. Their cotton crops were extremely abundant and workers were sorely needed. This boom for plantation owners caused an increase in the value of slaves. Slaves, however, continued to seek their freedom in escape from harsh masters to Northern states. Because slaves were increasing in value to the plantation owners, the plantation owners increased their efforts to keep their slaves. And when slaves ran away, plantation owners increased their efforts to get them back. As a result, slave owners would hire bounty hunters, often called slave catchers, to find their runaway slaves and bring them back. Great efforts were put into the retrieval of runaway slaves. Some plantation owners even went after the slaves themselves. As the Underground Railroad developed, slave catchers found that retrieving slaves became more and more difficult because of the distances slaves were able to run and the sophistication and organization of the escape routes. By 1850, with a majority of Congress still proslavery, heavy emphasis was put on the issue of slave loss. This resulted in the passage of the Fugitive Slave Law of 1850 (Putnam, 1907). This powerful law, slanted totally in favor of the plantation owners and against fugitive slaves, gave leeway to plantation owners to seek and find runaway slaves. They were even allowed to appeal to local authorities to help catch the runaways in order to return them to the plantations. The law also made it illegal for anyone to go against the return of slaves by assisting in their escapes. In fact, the law made it illegal to even withhold information without providing help. The law forced all citizens to help return all escaping slaves to plantation owners. Anyone who refused to assist authorities, or who helped slaves in any way, was subject to heavy penalties (Wisconsin History Society, n.d.) The Fugitive Slave Law of 1850 created even more antislavery feelings among citizens of Wisconsin. Both Wisconsin legislative houses voted against the passage of this law and political conventions in Waterford, Milwaukee, and Waukesha condemned the law. The Fugitive Slave Law of 1850 became a rallying point for abolitionists who felt morally compelled to disobey it and so became criminals in the eyes of the law (Wisconsin History Society, n.d.).

It is important to understand that the state circumstances in Wisconsin revealed a mirror of issues on a national level. The Fugitive Slave Law played a key role in the argumentation between Southern and Northern states over the idea of slavery. The fugitive slave clause of the original Constitution resulted in the Congressional Act of 1793 that allowed a federal or state judge to decide on claims made on a fugitive by a slave owner who was attempting to reclaim a slave (Niven, 1990, p. 62). As time went on and more people became opposed to slavery, Northern states, including Wisconsin, began passing what were called personal liberty laws. These laws sought to block the 1793 act and allow for accused slaves to be tried in free states to determine if rendition could occur (Niven, 1990, p. 62). The Fugitive Slave Act of 1793 was questioned in courts several times before the most famous case in the matter eventuated. In *Prigg v. Pennsylvania* in 1842, the United States Supreme Court upheld the Fugitive Slave Act (Niven, 1990, p. 63). In affirming that slave extraditions were exclusively a federal power, the decision also struck down states' rights in passing and exercising personal liberty laws.

As states continued to battle over slavery, splits in the union between the North and the South were carefully watched in terms of the decision as to whether or not to support slavery and the federal laws regarding slavery. When California and New Mexico were being considered for statehood, the intensity increased. In 1849, the United States consisted of 15 free states and 15 slave states. California's constitution prohibited slavery and thus it would enter the union as a free state. This would create a loss of balance at 16–15. Texas, a slave state, argued that the territory of New Mexico was an extension of the state of Texas and therefore should be slave territory (Todd and Curti, 1996, p. 355). Arguments regarding these issues led to the Compromise of 1850, engineered mainly by Henry Clay, which resulted in significant impacts for both free and slave states. California was added as a free state. The territories added from Mexico would operate under *popular sovereignty*, meaning that the people who moved to the territories would determine if they were free or slave. The Compromise of 1850 also held the position that a new fugitive slave law would be put into effect that would require state and local law enforcement officials to assist federal authorities in the capture and return of runaway slaves (Todd and Curti, 1996, p. 356). This new law became known as the Fugitive Slave Law of 1850. It put new force into an old argument and escalated abolitionists' activities against slavery and, in particular, rendition. The road to the Civil War, if not already established, was paved throughout the 1850s. The nation, in disagreement over slavery, was barely holding together.

Another act, the Kansas-Nebraska Act, added more controversy to the issue. Two more new territories were going to be added to the nation. Both of these territories were located north of the boundary line set up in the Missouri Compromise of 1820. That boundary line determined slave versus free territory. Senator Stephen Douglas sponsored the Kansas-Nebraska Act, which in effect repealed the Missouri Compromise and eliminated the boundary line. The result would be that popular sovereignty would be used to determine if the territories would be free or slave (Niven, 1990, pp. 79–115). Popular sovereignty was not a popular concept in either the South or the North. Southerners declared that the territories were common property and slavery couldn't be kept out. Northerners felt that popular sovereignty was an attempt to perpetuate slavery. Even more so, Northern states would see themselves as isolated free states within a sea of slave territories. Wisconsin and other Northern states vehemently opposed the Kansas-Nebraska Act on these grounds (Baker, 2006, p. 4).

This, then, is the background of the Wisconsin culture as it mirrored the national culture and arrived at a crucial moment on March 10, 1854. The Fugitive Slave Clause of the U.S. Constitution led to the passage of the Fugitive Slave Act of 1793. Tested in 1842 by *Prigg v. Pennsylvania*, the 1793 law was upheld and then strengthened in 1850 on the heels of the Compromise of 1850, which called for federal jurisdiction only and required state and local assistance to support slave rendition in free states. Also in 1854, the Kansas-Nebraska Act added to the heated arguments over slavery and the notion of popular sovereignty. In Wisconsin and other Northern states, the fear was that if free states had to accept slave property within their borders, it meant that owning slaves was within the law and protected by the U.S. Constitution and enforceable in all states (Baker, 2006, pp. 4–5). In this scenario, nothing would prevent slave owners from permanently bringing their slaves to free states.

Joshua Glover arrived in Racine in 1852. Prior to that, he had been living and working as a slave in St. Louis (Olin, 1893). He decided he had had enough of slavery and ran away to the free state of Wisconsin. Descriptions of Glover's actual physical appearance vary with different sources. In the warrant for his arrest, he was described as about 44 or 45 years old with large hands and feet, prominent knuckles, and a full head of "wool." He was listed as five feet six inches tall with long legs and a thin body. He was noted as having an ashy black color with small and inflamed eyes (Baker, 2006, p. 66). After his arrest and during trials that resulted from his release, witnesses described him as 30–45 years old, five feet ten inches tall, and dark brown with all the other features being the same as mentioned above (Baker, 2006, p. 66). The reward advertisement poster put out by his owner after he had runaway but before his arrest described him as 38–40 years old and six feet tall with all the other features being the same (Two Hundred Dollars Reward, 1852, p. 1). No photos of Glover are known to exist. There is, however, a portrait from the 1880s that is popularly used as the caricature of Joshua Glover (Wisconsin Electric Reader, n.d.). This portrait most likely does not reflect what Glover actually looked like but has been accepted as a symbol of his story.

Probably hearing about the proabolitionist sentiment in and around the city of Racine and Racine County in general, Glover decided to settle, not actually in Racine, but four miles outside of the city. He obtained a job at a local sawmill owned by Duncan Sinclair. Sinclair also provided a cabin of his for Glover to use as living quarters (Baker, 2006, p. 2). All things considered, it seemed like things were going well for Glover. With a place to live and a steady job, Glover also found time to work at his own carpentry skills. He became quite talented and enjoyed making his own handcrafted items. Occasionally, Glover would travel the four miles into Racine to sell his work as a freelancer. He was good enough to be noticed for his talents (Baker, 2006, p. 2).

Glover had few friends. This is not unusual for a Black man from the South now living in the North. Keeping a low profile was standard operating procedure not only for runaway slaves but for their abolitionist supporters as well. It was well known that slave owners often came north to look for their runaway slaves. It was also well known that bounty hunters were hired by Southern slave owners to retrieve their slaves. The battles over popular sovereignty, states' rights, and slavery were not clearly delineated and laws led Blacks to believe there would be major complications if they were retrieved, even in free states. Abolitionists and fugitives alike knew full well when slave catchers were in the area and both used low profiles as a normal defense against recognition. No one wanted to be noticed or to draw attention to themselves or their cause. Most likely for all of these reasons, as far as is known, Glover limited himself to just three friends. There was a woman whose name has not survived history and two men, William Alby and Nelson Turner (Baker, 2006, p. 2). It is not known if these two men worked with Glover or worked at all. Turner had freedom papers and was up from Natchez, Mississippi (Baker, 2006, p. 1). Not much is known about Alby or the woman.

On Friday night March 10, 1854, Joshua Glover was relaxing in his cabin with his two friends, Alby and Turner. They were playing cards and talking when a knock came at the door. Always careful to lock his door, Glover was especially careful on this night because of what had happened the day before. United States Marshals had visited Glover's cabin on Thursday. Glover was not at home, but as the marshals approached, Glover's woman friend, who thought the marshals were after her, beat it out the back door and ran away. She was never seen again. The marshals left empty handed then but they came back the next day. When the knock on the door occurred, Glover told Alby and Turner not to go near the door. Turner ignored Glover and quickly unlocked the door (Baker, 2006, pp. 1–2). What happened next was not surprising.

Upon the door being unlocked, seven men rushed in. Bennami Garland, the man who claimed Glover as his slave, had enlisted the aid of two U.S. Deputy Marshals and four assistants to sneak up on Glover's cabin and capture Glover. How they knew where Glover was is a mystery but there is the suggestion that Nelson Turner was the one who betrayed Glover (Baker, 2006, p. 1), probably for money. Garland had done more than the minimum of legal work to arrange for the rendering of his slave. He had gone to court in St. Louis and had proven he was the legal owner of Glover and that Glover had run away in 1852 (Baker, 2006, p. 1). In addition, he had posted a reward announcement of $200 in the *St. Louis Missouri Republican* newspaper naming Glover as a runaway slave (Two Hundred Dollars Reward, 1852, p. 1). By law, he also had to convince the judge in St. Louis that he had credible information that Glover was living near Racine (Baker, 2006, p. 1). Again, it would appear that Turner provided this information, which seems to explain why he immediately unlocked the cabin door. The St. Louis court issued Garland a certificate of removal, which made it legal for him to pursue Glover (Baker, 2006, p. 1). Upon retrieving Glover, Garland, according to law, only had to appear before a federal judge or commissioner in Wisconsin and present his certificate and make a case that the person he had retrieved was the one he was authorized to retrieve. This usually was not a difficult task as almost any evidence presented was accepted (Baker, 2006, p. 2). Garland even went so far as to obtain a warrant for Glover's arrest from U.S. District Judge Andrew Miller of the Eastern District of Wisconsin (Baker, 2006, p. 2). Garland was taking no chances on the retrieval of his slave.

According to Baker (2006), when the men stormed the cabin no documents of arrest were shared as Glover immediately fought against the odds for his freedom (p. 2). At first only three men attacked him, but as he was not controlled by these three men, even with a gun pointed to his head, the others joined the fray and eventually the seven of them were able to subdue Glover and put him in manacles. During the fight, William Alby jumped out a window and ran to Racine to report what had happened (Baker, 2006, p. 2). Reports of the arrest leave out the fate of Nelson Turner. Mention of his whereabouts from the arrest forward is absent. What happened to Glover, Garland, and the two U.S. Deputy Marshals is known. Deputy Marshal John Kearney, who had knocked Glover down by striking him with a cudgel (Baker, 2006, p. 2), and his assistant Daniel F. Houghton went back to Racine from where they had come. By the time they arrived back in Racine, Alby had alerted abolitionists who were already stirring about the arrest (Baker, 2006, p. 2). Kearney and Houghton were met by hundreds of abolitionists who had demanded that the Racine County sheriff question them as to what had happened and as to where Glover was. When they refused to provide the information, Sheriff Timothy D. Morris arrested them (Baker, 2006, pp. 2–3).

Baker (2006) reports that Glover, Garland, and Deputy Marshal Charles Cotton did not go back to Racine (p. 3). They knew Racine was a thoroughly proabolitionist town and would not support the slave rendering of Joshua Glover. Wisely, from their point of view, they headed overnight to travel the thirty miles to Milwaukee, as previously noted, a not-so-abolitionist town. They knew they would be better received in this bigger less-sensitive town than they would be in Racine. They also knew there were other advantages. First, a larger town would make it easier for them to do their work covertly (Baker, 2006, p. 3). More importantly, Judge Miller's seat was in Milwaukee as was the seat of U.S. Commissioner for Wisconsin, Winfield Smith (Baker, 2006, p. 3). Their plan was to immediately seek permission by either of these judges to remove Glover from Wisconsin and take him back to Missouri (Baker, 2006, p. 3). It took them most of the night to get back to Milwaukee. Upon their arrival, they put Glover in the Milwaukee County Jail. He was still bleeding from the injuries he had received. No doctor had been called to treat Glover's wounds.

By Saturday morning, Racine was in a frenzy regarding the arrest of Joshua Glover. Reportedly, a thousand or more people assembled and came out to the courthouse to address the issue (Olin, 1893). Calling it a kidnapping, they resolved to condemn the attackers, assure Glover a fair trial, and declare that the citizens of Wisconsin considered the Fugitive Slave Law of 1850 repealed. They sent their resolutions by telegraph to well-known abolitionist printer Sherman Booth in Milwaukee. Booth was known as an excitable man, Yale-educated, and antislavery through and through (Baker, 2006, p. 6).

Baker's account (2006) describes that when Booth got the telegram from Racine, he went directly to see Judge Miller (p. 8). Hurrying to see the judge, Booth met Marshall Cotton and confronted him regarding the kidnapping of Joshua Glover. Cotton stated that he had not kidnapped Glover and that apparently ended the discussion at that point. When he spoke to Judge Miller, Booth found out that Miller had written an arrest warrant a few days earlier (Baker, 2006, p. 8). Leaving Miller's office, Booth met with well-known abolitionist lawyer, James Paine. Paine had heard of the arrest and was rushing to the county jail. Booth went with him. Finding Glover in the county jail, Paine took a statement regarding the arrest from Glover. He also obtained a copy of the arrest warrant. Having these in hand, Paine then went to see Milwaukee County Judge, Charles E. Jenkins. He applied to Judge Jenkins for a writ of habeas corpus for Joshua Glover and Jenkins issued the writ and ordered the city marshals to serve it on the federal marshals and the county sheriff who held Glover (Baker, 2006, pp. 8–9).

Baker (2006), reports that at 1:00 Booth, Paine, and others met in Booth's printing office to discuss the situation (p. 10). They telegraphed the abolitionists in Racine to tell them what had occurred to that point. No one believed that Judge Miller was going to abide by the writ of habeas corpus. They all figured Miller would hold a hearing for Garland and arrange a quick removal of Glover to Missouri. Based on this belief, they decided to call a general meeting at the county courthouse (Baker, 2006, p. 10). The call went out by word of mouth, by the ringing of church bells, and by Booth printing handbills publicizing Glover's arrest (Baker, 2006, p. 10). In the handbills, Booth claimed that slavecatchers had kidnapped a man and had him tied up at the county jail. Further, he claimed in the handbills that the slave owner would not have a public trial but would secretly take the kidnapped man away without benefit of council (Baker, 2006, p. 9). Booth urged citizens to not accept a man being "dragged back to slavery" from Wisconsin's free soil without open trial to his personal right to liberty (Baker, 2006, p. 9). Pressed for time, Booth got on his horse and raced around town distributing the handbills and shouting "A man's liberty is at stake" (Baker, 2006, p. 10). People all over town stopped to hear the story. By 2:30, he had finished his plea to the people and as the call had gone out, as many as 5000 people had responded by gathering at the courthouse (Baker, 2006, pp. 10, 86–87). This huge crowd of people included citizens of all walks of life including city officials, successful business owners, and curious citizens. A quiet court proceeding to remove Glover was no longer possible (Baker, 2006, p. 10).

It was not unusual for large gatherings to take place at a common location throughout towns in the territories and states. It was still a new nation and Wisconsin was still a very new state. In cities and towns across the United States, people were interpreting the laws set up in the Constitution as they pertained to their locale. The interpretation of the Federal Constitution in relation to states' rights was a particularly sensitive issue. In the Glover case in 1854, it was to be expected that a slave removal via federal law in a free state would rub up against the interpretation of states' rights in giving up that slave. Arguments regarding this basic dilemma ran along several lines.

In Milwaukee, popular sovereignty was an issue, especially with abolitionists. Several basic questions were being considered. Did the people of Wisconsin wish to allow a person to be considered a fugitive slave on the free soil of Wisconsin? Did the people of Wisconsin support the removal of fugitive slaves from Wisconsin free soil? Did the people of Wisconsin wish to have federal marshals, judges, and commissioners decide law on the issue of slavery in Wisconsin? Though states' rights obviously played a huge role, the crux of the matter most likely came down to proslavery versus antislavery, not only in Wisconsin but in the nation. In this regard, Wisconsin mirrored a nation heading to the brink of civil war.

Several abolitionist speakers delivered messages to the crowd regarding what had happened with Glover. James Paine called the meeting to order and several notable citizens were nominated and elected to conduct the meeting. Dr. Edward B. Wolcott, an extremely well-known and popular businessman with diverse interests in the community was elected president (Baker, 2006, p. 17). Abram Henry Bielfield, a wealthy German immigrant and popular with local politicians, was elected secretary (Baker, 2006, p. 17). Committees were formed to create resolutions (Booth and Paine included). James Paine's son, Byron, was called upon to review the legalities of the case and quickly became a highly-respected leader in the event (Baker, 2006, p. 18). Paine fed into antislavery enthusiasm by declaring the Fugitive Slave Law unconstitutional because it denied the right of the writ of habeas corpus guaranteed by both the federal and state constitutions (Baker, 2006, p. 19). Even more important was Paine's insistence that law emanated from popular sovereignty (Baker, 2006, p. 19). This meant the people had the right to decide on Glover's fate as the Fugitive Slave Law was interpreted by the people in its application in Wisconsin.

Meanwhile, both legal and political reasons created interesting circumstances for the law enforcement officials involved in the case. U.S. Deputy Marshal Cotton was holding a federal prisoner who was arrested on a warrant from a U.S. District Judge. The complication for Cotton was that he had now been served a writ of habeas corpus by the local city marshal who demanded that he explain his arrest. Milwaukee County Sheriff Page was under little pressure because Wisconsin law stated that he had to accept federal prisoners but couldn't release them. When Cotton went to Judge Miller for directions on what to do, Miller told him to ignore the warrant (Baker, 2006, p. 18).

As the meeting carried on for several hours that Saturday afternoon, the fervor of the event escalated as speakers claimed popular sovereignty, states' rights, and the unconstitutionality of the Fugitive Slave Law. Deputy Marshal Cotton worried about the crowd enough to order the local militia to protect prisoner Glover (Baker, 2006, p. 21). In addition, U.S. District Attorney for Wisconsin John Sharpstein arrived in Milwaukee to investigate the arrest of Glover. Sharpstein ordered the federal battalion stationed in the area to protect the prisoner. Neither the local militia nor the battalion showed up to protect the prisoner (Baker, 2006, p. 21), thus apparently indicating how they felt about the arrest.

The leaders of the general meeting (perhaps at Byron Paine's indirect suggestion) ordered another writ of habeas corpus for Cotton (Baker, 2006, p. 21). After the writ was received, this writ was also taken by Cotton to Miller who again advised Cotton to ignore it. By now, everyone on the federal side believed the crowd would take the prisoner if the prisoner was moved from the jail to the courthouse. Though the jail was adjacent to the courthouse, the crowd was on the courthouse grounds and a taking of the prisoner would not be difficult. The assembly at this time was still within the law, still peaceful, and still had committed no violent acts. The federal officials were not sure they would stay that way if the prisoner was moved. In addition, the assembly committees brought forth three petitions with resolutions approved by the assembly as a whole. These resolutions demanded that a fair trial be put forth for the personal liberty of the prisoner, that the writ of habeas corpus be carried out, and that the assembly would stand by the prisoner (Baker, 2006, p. 20). A vigilance committee was created to watch the jail and the courthouse to better enable the resolutions to be met. Members of this committee included lawyers Byron Paine and Edward Palmer as well as local businessmen John Furlong, John Ryecraft, and Herbert Reed (Baker, 2006, p. 22). The situation was getting intense.

At 5:00 as the second writ was being delivered and rejected, the steamboat ferry from Racine arrived. The assembly that gathered in Racine over the arrest of Glover had resulted in 100 abolitionists taking the afternoon ferry to Milwaukee to support the Milwaukeeans who opposed the arrest (Olin, 1893). As they arrived at the dock, they became immediately aware of the Milwaukee assembly at the courthouse and proceeded to march there without hesitation. The Racine crowd was orderly and peaceful. With the arrival of the Racine abolitionists, a renewed eagerness regarding the situation developed (Legler, 1898). The assembly's investigators had found out about the calls to local and federal troops. They feared that this meant that Glover would be taken away by these forces. A rumor began circulating that Glover would be removed that very evening in spite of Judge Miller putting out news that Glover would get a fair trial on Monday morning. The committee began to believe that some plan was underfoot to undermine their resolutions. Aware of the spirit within the ranks, assembly leaders began responding to the crowd by delivering fiery speeches regarding citizens needing to take the law into their own hands at times. In particular, a lawyer named Charles Watkins and Sherman Booth spoke of citizens taking the law into their own hands sometimes. Booth emphasized that this would be one way to express the idea that the Fugitive Slave Law was unconstitutional. Baker (p. 22) reports that both men coyly stated that they didn't know if this was such a time for citizens to take the law into their own hands. Booth, especially, urged the crowd to break no laws, but by now the crowd had been riled. The assembly was on the edge of taking action. As Watkins and Booth left for dinner, the crowd left for Glover.

James Angove is the man who is identified for leading the assembly's way to the courthouse. Once there, 100 men stormed the jailhouse and asked the officer in charge of the jail for the keys to get in (Legler, 1898). The officer refused and James Angove used a piece of wood to lead others with pickaxes to break down the door to the jail. None of the men guarding Glover was assaulted in any way or held or even threatened (Baker, 2006, p. 23). And seeing the size of the crowd, they offered no defense of the prisoner's release. The federal marshals present were helpless, knew it, and did nothing as Glover was released and taken to a horse and buggy owned by local businessman, John Messinger (Helped Save Glover, 1900, p. 2). The scene was wild as Glover doffed his cap, cried "Glory Hallelujah," and rode away with Messenger driving and Sherman Booth on horseback next to the buggy (Baker, 2006, p. 23). Glover was headed for a trip on the Wisconsin Underground Railroad beginning at Waukesha, continuing to Racine, and culminating in Canada

(Baker, 2006, p. 23). Glover rode out of sight and was gone forever, never to return to Wisconsin or Missouri.

The assembly's actions regarding the release of Joshua Glover have close association with the circumstances which mirrored the nation during the turbulent times leading to the Civil War. Most argued was the notion of legal assembly. General speaking, citizens and officials alike believed that the assembly was legal up to the jailbreak. Newspapers of the time report these findings while arguing back and forth as to whether the nonviolent nature of the jailbreak allowed even that part of the situation to be legal (Baker, 2006, pp. 23–24). A bigger argument was if the assembly had the right under popular sovereignty to interpret the democratic process so far as to free Glover.

Playing into the local situation were the events being played out on the bigger stage of the entire nation. The Fugitive Slave Clause of the U.S. Constitution leading to the passage of the Fugitive Slave Act of 1793 exploded into the Fugitive Slave Law of 1850. The explosion was kindled along the way by the Missouri Compromise of 1820, the *Prigg v. Pennsylvania* decision of 1842, the Compromise of 1850, and related thinking by the legislators and the general citizenry regarding slavery, states' rights, and federal law. Following the passage of the Fugitive Slave Law of 1850, bills such as the Kansas-Nebraska Act introduced more arguments into the national controversy, especially regarding popular sovereignty as it related to slavery. The volatile atmosphere, which would eventually lead to widespread social upheaval, caused controversy over the release of Joshua Glover to carry on for years, all the way to the beginning of the Civil War.

As reported in part by Legler (1898) and in detail by Baker in the fourth chapter of his book (Baker, 2006, pp. 80–111), soon after Joshua Glover disappeared into Canada suits and countersuits began and carried on for nearly seven years. Lawyers for both sides were many but the principle players were James Paine, Byron Paine, Charles Watkins, John Sharpstein, Caleb Cushing, and Edward G. Ryan. There were several judges involved as well with the primary ones remaining to be Judges Miller and Smith. Dozens of witnesses both within and without the assembly were called and recalled. A broad overview culled from Baker's chapter of court proceedings throughout the years found the following suits and countersuits.

Garland sued Booth to compensate his loss of property. The federal government indicted Booth and Ryecraft for the jailbreak. Garland was arrested for kidnapping and assault and battery against Glover. Judge Miller freed Garland. Booth was arrested for helping Glover disappear. Booth lost his trial regarding the jailbreak and was held. Garland sued Booth a second time for loss of property. This time he sought $4000. As Booth began losing his printing property to lawsuits, antislavery meetings continued to be called. Congressional elections and U.S. Senate appointments were added to popular resistance as successful methods of fostering antislavery attitudes and a quest for repealing the Fugitive Slave Law of 1850. Abram Smith of the Wisconsin Supreme Court ruled the Fugitive Slave Law unconstitutional and freed Booth. The decision was upheld by the full Wisconsin Supreme Court after Sharpstein appealed the original ruling. In spite of this, Ryecraft was brought to trial and was found guilty on charges regarding the jailbreak. He served ten days in jail and paid a $1000 fine and court costs (Legler, 1898). Walcott, Watkins, both Paines, and others were indicted in the escape. Booth was retried and found guilty in the jailbreak. He was rearrested and sentenced to one month in jail and a fine of $1000 plus court costs (Legler, 1900). In 1857, Wisconsin passed and enacted a law to prevent kidnapping. The purpose of the law was to prevent the capture of slaves seeking asylum in the state (Legler, 1898). On March 3, 1861, Booth was pardoned by President Buchanan. On June 25, 1864, the Fugitive Slave Law was repealed.

Joshua Glover spent the last 34 years of his life in freedom in Canada. He was able to seek and find employment with Thomas Montgomery. Montgomery operated an inn and also operated a large farming property. Joshua Glover died in 1888 at the York County Industrial Home/County House in Newmarket, Ontario, Canada (Olin, 1893).

Glossary

Compromise of 1850: This legislation included arguments on several issues relating to the spread of slavery in territories that would be added as states and motivated the Fugitive Slave Law of 1850.

Congressional Act of 1793: This act called for the amendment of the U.S. Constitution to allow for the right of owners to recover escaped slaves.

Cudgel: A short stick used as a weapon.

Free Soil: Another name for free states in which slavery was prohibited.

Fugitive Slave Act of 1793: In response to the U.S. Constitution, this act gave slave owners the legal right to recover escaped slaves.

Fugitive Slave Law of 1850: According to this law, marshals and citizens could not, by penalty of law, in any way hinder or hide the capture, arrest, and return of all fugitive slaves.

Kansas-Nebraska Act: This act annulled the Missouri Compromise and provided for the organization of the territories of Kansas and Nebraska and permitting these territories self-determination on the question of slavery.

Manacles: A metal band, chain, or shackle for fastening someone's hands or ankles.

Missouri Compromise of 1820: This act allowed Missouri to be admitted to the union as a slave state, Maine to be admitted as a free state, and for slavery to be permitted in the Louisiana Purchase north of latitude 36'30'N except for Missouri.

Prigg v. Pennsylvania: The U.S. Supreme Court case in 1842 that declared all fugitive slave laws enacted by states unconstitutional and made federal law the guiding hand of fugitive slave issues.

Slave Catchers: People who tracked down, captured, and returned slaves to their owners for a bounty.

States' Rights: Rights or powers held by states rather than held by the federal government.

Writ of Habeas Corpus: A court order that commands an individual or a government official who has restrained an individual to produce that individual at a designated time and a designated place so that a court can determine the legality of the restraint and to decide whether to order the individual released.

Discussion/Reflection

1. Was Garland justified in hunting down and capturing Glover? If so, explain why. If not, explain why not.
2. Using facts to support your viewpoint, describe your opinion of the Fugitive Slave Law of 1850.
3. How do you think Garland knew where Glover was? What in the chapter makes you think so?
4. What are your opinions regarding the actions of the police and legal authorities during the arrest, while Glover was incarcerated, and in preparation for the trial? Do you think they acted within the law?
5. What are your opinions regarding the actions of Booth and Paine? Do you think they were acting out of commitment to a cause or for personal gain? Explain.
6. What do you think motivated James Angrove? Could you have led the charge as he did?
7. Choose any moment along the way and tell what you think Glover was thinking and how he felt.
8. Most people see the assembly as legal up until the jailbreak. Many people believe that even the jailbreak was legal under popular sovereignty. Some people question if the assembly had the right under

popular sovereignty to interpret the democratic process as far as to free Glover. What do you think? Be sure to use details to support your response.
9. In what ways does Joshua Glover's story relate to immigrants around the world today?
10. Share a story of someone you know who may have experienced some part of what Glover experienced.

Selected Topics for Further Study

1. Fur traders in early American history
2. African American populations in your state and geographic location and history
3. Fugitive Slave Act of 1793
4. *Prigg v. Pennsylvania*
5. Free states and slave states
6. The Compromise of 1850
7. Henry Clay
8. Kansas-Nebraska Act
9. Missouri Compromise of 1820
10. Popular sovereignty
11. Racine, Wisconsin
12. Bounty hunters
13. Federal district court system
14. Sherman Booth
15. Byron Paine
16. States' rights
17. Citizen's rights within the law
18. Legal assembly
19. President Buchanan
20. Thomas Montgomery

References

Baker, H. Robert (2006). *The rescue of Joshua Glover: A fugitive slave, the Constitution, and the coming of the Civil War*. Athens, OH: Ohio University Press.

"Helped save Glover." Milwaukee Sentinel, June 10, 1900. Retrieved from http://www.wisconsinhistory.org/turningpoints/search.asp?id=1033

Legler, Henry E. (1898). Rescue of Joshua Glover: A runaway slave, Wisconsin Electronic Reader. Retrieved from http://www.library.wisc.edu/etext/WIReader/WER1124.html

Murrell, James (2004). Underground Railroad ran through Wisconsin. *The Madison Times*. Retrieved from http://www.madtimes.com/archives/feb2004_3/top_story1.htm

Niven, John (1990). *The coming of the Civil War: 1837–1861*. Wheeling, IL: Harlan Davidson.

Olin, Chauncy C. (1893). The Olin Album. Burlington Historical Society. Retrieved from http://www.burlingtonhistory.org/joshua_glover.htm

Pferdehirt, Julia (1998). *Freedom train north: Stories of the Underground Railroad in Wisconsin*. Middleton, WI: Living History Press.

Putnam, Dora (1907). The Underground Railway in Wisconsin. *Waukesha Freeman*. Retrieved from http://www.wisconsinhistory.org/turningpoints/search.asp?id=1560

Todd, Lewis Paul and Merle Curti (1966). *Rise of the American nation*, 2nd ed. NY: Harcourt, Brace & World.

Wisconsin Electronic Reader (n.d.). Joshua Glover: The fugitive slave. Retrieved from http://www.wisconsinhistory.org/turningpoints/search.asp?id=1562

Wisconsin Historical Society. (n.d.). The Underground Railroad in Wisconsin. Retrieved from http://www.wisconsinhistory.org/Content.aspx?dsNav=N:4294963828-4294963805&dsRecordDetailS=R:CS566

· 3 ·

THE BIRTH OF THE NATIONAL ASSOCIATION OF COLORED WOMEN'S CLUBS

> "This was the first time that colored women have been given the decided recognition in a social way by a woman of lighter skin."
> —Chicago Times Herald, 1899

By the nineteenth century, women's roles in American society had been quite clearly established. They were subordinate. Based in part on the religious upbringings of the nation, women found their place beneath men regarding personal/social class status and indeed in nearly every identifiable category. They could not enter the professions; they could not own a business; they could not vote in elections; they could not keep accounts; they could not go places and do things that men did; they could not express ideas or opinions outside of the home. In short, they had no voice. Their place within the family itself was indicative of their place within society. If there was a place for the voice of women, surely it was in the home. By the seventeenth century, early Americans had already determined that women were natural nurturers and teachers, morally more uplifting than men and, thus, better equipped to do the child rearing. However, according to a study conducted regarding the role of the colonial family (Demos, 1970, pp. 183–186), women were found to be subordinate to men based on the premise "He for God only, she for God in him" (Spring 2011). Historian Joel Spring (2011) interprets this to mean that women were to bow to the God in men, and men were to assume the spiritual care of women (p. 39). In legal matters, the married woman was at the mercy of her husband; she was without rights to own property, make contracts, or sue for damages. Surely, this subordinate status put women in a position of unequal footing with regard to nearly every facet of life, including personal/social status, with the exception of child rearing, which men clearly called upon women to undertake and within which, by and large, they excelled (Spring, 2011).

If the above describes the conditions for White women in American society in the nineteenth century, imagine what conditions were like for African American women, who were clearly looked upon as beneath the status of both White men and White women. The combined issues of gender role and race role perceived by American society of the 1800s were such that African American women were relegated to the lowest position. Their rights, privileges, and opportunities were limited to an even further degree than White women simply because of their skin color. As if this was not enough, the one bastion of civility for White women, leadership role in family child rearing, was affected for African American women by dominant culture attitudes as well. Although African American women excelled at child rearing as did White women, their opportunity to do so was much more difficult. Indeed, the nature and disorganization of slave families were breeding grounds for dysfunction because family members were sold at the discretion of the slave owner, marriages dissolved, and fathers disappeared because they were sold or killed, or perhaps just ran away.

This subordinate status of women, both White and Black, led necessarily to increased efforts on the parts of courageous and dedicated leaders to obtain an equal ground for women in American status. Though their paths are interwoven and finally joined, White women and Black women weave their way toward equal rights from different perspectives and on different plains. Certain people, events, and groups have contributed immensely to the progress that has been made by both groups since the beginning of the nineteenth century. Surely, the birth of the National Association of Colored Women's Clubs (NACWC) has not been the total picture of status reform for American women, particularly African American women; however, the NACWC plays a significant and symbolic role in the development of women's, and thus humans', rights in America since the 1800s. The work of the NACWC and the organizations it grew out of and spawned provides a picture of the issues that were addressed on the way to increased status for women, in particular, African American women.

The Women's Rights Movement began in 1848 in Seneca Falls, New York. It was there that a convention of men and women was held to discuss the rights of women. In fact, some of the earliest leaders in the women's movement attended the convention. Sojourner Truth, Elizabeth Cady Stanton, William Wells Brown, Charles Lenox Remond, and Frederick Douglass all attended and took leadership roles at this convention. Douglass had previously written in his publication *North Star* that "Right is of no sex" (Wesely, 1984, p. 2). The right being discussed at this convention was the right to vote. It was Elizabeth Cady Stanton who made the motion that "It is the duty of women in this country to secure themselves their sacred right to the election franchise" (Wesely, 1984, p. 2). Notably, the motion was seconded by Frederick Douglass, who would go on to become an icon of the movement and a revered figure in the NACWC. Stanton and other members of this first convention, Lucretia Mott and Susan B. Anthony, were leaders in the formation of the National Women's Suffrage Association (NWSA) in 1851. They had organized conferences and conventions throughout the 1840s that dealt with a multiplicity of women's issues but mostly voting rights. By 1866, NWSA changed its name to the Equal Rights Association in order to identify its main ambition more clearly. The objective of the group remained that of universal suffrage. These early examples of organizations are indicators of the beginning of efforts toward women's rights. However, even before the 1840s, there were significant numbers of societies and clubs formed on local levels by African American women. Most of these were antislavery and literary societies that brought local women together to address local concerns. On December 4, 1833, for example, the American Anti-Slavery Society was formed. The importance of this group was in its encouragement of women into its membership (Black and White) and the work it did to establish schools, to campaign against the Fugitive Slave Laws, and to assist in the Underground Railroad. The agendas of these groups included a heavy emphasis on moral and religious issues to guide people to live their lives honestly and in a wholesome fashion. The importance of morality and religion was interwoven with the importance of education, especially literacy. Education was encouraged most strongly for children, but it was encouraged also for adults.

Typically, societies, or clubs, were located in the northern so-called free states. White women who joined the antislavery cause were Lucretia Mott, Abby Kelly Foster, Lucy Stone, and Susan B. Anthony. One African

American spokesperson of the time, author Fannie Barrier Williams, declared that "Among colored women, the club is the effort of the few competent on the behalf of the many incompetent" (Wesely, 1984, p. 2). Her statement is historically accurate as a cadre of well-identified, competent women assumed leadership positions and attempted to uplift others while they climbed into better positions themselves. This early observation connects clearly with African American women escalating the importance of the African American traditional values of education by attending colleges in higher numbers throughout the mid-1800s. In fact, most of the NACWC's key leaders were college graduates. Other Black women who led the antislavery cause were Francis Ellen, Watkins Harper, Sojourner Truth, Harriet Tubman, and Amanda Smith. These early church clubs became the models for the proliferation of later local club work, which by the end of the century would gain great speed and produce great numbers of clubs both locally and statewide with thousands of members.

In New York City in the 1860s, a women's club was formed to investigate ways to further the causes of women. This club of White women was called the Sorosis Club. For its twenty-first anniversary celebration, this club sent out a call to approximately 100 other women's clubs inviting them to send delegates to its convention in New York City. On March 20, 1889, 61 clubs represented by over 100 delegates met to form the Federation of Women's Clubs (FWC). A constitution was adopted the next year and conventions were begun on a biennial basis beginning in 1892. The FWC became the first national organization of women's clubs. Though its constitution, written in 1890, did not allow the admittance of African Americans, not much was made of it until 1899. In spite of this drawback, the FWC became a subtle motivating factor for the eventual organization of the NACWC. Other events had been and were occurring to advance Black women's causes. Throughout the 1860s, 1870s, and 1880s, higher education institutions such as Oberlin College, Fisk University, Wilberforce College, Wellesley College, Vassar, Cornell, Howard University, Atlanta University, Chicago University, and others had not only been admitting Black women, but they were also graduating them. In 1862, Mary Jane Patterson became the first Black woman to graduate from Oberlin College. Mary Church Terrell, Anna Julia Cooper, and Ida Gibbs graduated in 1884. Spelman College for Black women opened in 1881. These colleges and their graduates opened the doors to many professions for women who from this time on began joining the ranks of nurses, physicians, lawyers, teachers, musicians, authors, editors, columnists, and businesswomen. The women who served as these examples also provided motivation for the organizations of hundreds of Black women's clubs on local levels and then state levels to consider community and state issues and to advance the establishment of education systems for the purposes of uplifting the oppressed masses. In addition to these goals and their desire to be morally uplifting, the clubs emphasized equality of opportunity with men and suffrage. While there were White women's clubs, which were willing and able to work with Black women's clubs to gain equality together, the most common occurrence was the increased formation of separate Black women's clubs in local communities which would over time evolve into state organizations and which would eventually develop the National Association of Colored Women's Clubs. For all practical purposes, though there were multiple exceptions on both sides, White women's clubs and Black women's clubs were developing separately. By the 1890s, local clubs and state organizations were headed toward national affiliation in both groups.

Among the many, some of the early leaders in organizing Black women's clubs on local and state levels included Josephine St. Pierre Ruffin, Hallie Quinn Brown, Mary Church Terrell, Victoria Earle Mathews, Josephine Silone Yates, Fannie Jackson Coppin, Margaret Murray Washington, and Agnes Jones Adams (Weseley, 1984).

Josephine St. Pierre Ruffin was a charter member of the Massachusetts School Suffrage Association and worked diligently with Lucy Stone and Julia Ward Howe in issues of universal suffrage. She was a member of 10 state women's clubs and an officer in most. These clubs were active in women's rights issues and they led Ruffin to establish a major national contributor to Black women's clubs, the Women's New Era Club, established in 1893. With her daughter Florida, she also started an important publication, *Woman's Era* magazine. She is credited with calling the first organizing convention of Black women, which resulted in the later calling of the first meeting of the National Association of Colored Women's Clubs.

Hallie Quinn Brown began her career as a teacher after having graduated from Wilberforce College in 1873. After a few years of teaching, she became very active in public speaking and traveled extensively as an elocutionist. After becoming well known as an elocutionist, Brown returned to Wilberforce as a professor and again traveled extensively on behalf of the college. In addition to her many travels in America, she traveled to Europe (as did several other Black women at that time) where her ideas of universal suffrage and equal rights for African Americans were well received. Strongly aligned with the Women's Christian Temperance Union and espousing their beliefs,

Hallie Q. Brown played a prominent role in the push for national recognition by helping to set the national stage. Much later, she became the seventh president of the NACWC and served from 1920 to 1924.

Mary Church Terrell was one of the first women to be on a board of education in America and was the first African American woman to serve. She attended Oberlin College and in 1885 became a professor at Wilberforce College. Attending various suffrage group meetings, Terrell became very interested in women's clubs and would become a force well after the turn of the century. She served on a number of committees including the International Congress of Women, the International League of Peace, and the Women's International League of Peace and Freedom. She founded the College Alumnae Club and served as its first president. During World War I she served as the National Supervisor of Work for the War Camp Community Service. She also served on the Republican National Committee. Unafraid to challenge other women's groups, Terrell led a fight against the American Association of University Women regarding its stance supporting school segregation. In part to indicate her defiance to some of the powerful male leaders of African Americans, she was a charter member of the National Association for the Advancement of Colored People. In 1896, she was elected first president of the National Association of Colored Women's Clubs. She was reelected twice.

In 1892 Victoria Earle Mathews formed the Women's Loyal Union of New York and Brooklyn. Becoming its first president, Mathews worked tirelessly for morality, social justice, and education for African American women. She responded to the call made by Ruffin in 1895. As she did with her own club from 1892 to 1895, Mathews became an extremely active member of the NACWC, attending lectures, reading, and enjoining women to their causes. She served as chairperson of the executive board and as National Organizer for the NACWC. Some of her most enthusiastic work went into programs such as the Traveler's Aid Society, the White Rose Mission, kindergarten formation, community women's clubs, and the Home for Colored Working Girls. All of these initiatives focused on the moral and healthy care of young girls and women, especially those young girls and women alone in urban areas and subject to the prey of deceitful people.

Josephine Silone Yates was the only African American graduate of the Rhode Island State Normal School in 1879. She became an editorial writer for newspapers and wrote widely of numerous facets of life in America, including the lives of women. She established herself as a leader in the Kansas City

Women's League in 1893. This involvement began her activity in local women's clubs. She used this local experience to become an avid supporter of the movement, which led to the organization of the NACWC. Attending nearly every meeting and serving on numerous committees, she played a large role in the national agenda and was elected as the organization's second president in 1900. At one point in her life, she studied under Fannie Jackson Coppin.

Fannie Jackson Coppin graduated from Oberlin College in 1865. She began her teaching career at the Institute for Colored Youth in Philadelphia. Soon she became principal of the school and served in that capacity for 40 years. During that time of great educational/social change, she established the Women's Industrial Exchange, where the works of her students were displayed. She became involved in local women's clubs, spoke at NACWC national conventions, and took her place in history as a pioneer of the women's club movement.

Margaret Murray Washington attended Fisk University and began her teaching career in 1889 at Tuskegee Institute. Serving as both teacher and dean of women, Washington immersed herself in community work, home visitations, the comprehensive work of church and schools, and the ideas and philosophies of her future husband. After marrying Booker T. Washington, she established the Tuskegee Women's Club and served as its president for the rest of her life. As with many leading women of the club movement, her main focus was the perpetuation of high ideals for education and community life. Her endless work and popularity were pivotal in getting her elected as president of the Alabama State Federation of Colored Women. The goals of this organization were to support reform schools for Black boys, to support schools in jails for prisoners, and to support the establishment of schools for girls. Washington's work became well known and supported across the South. She became president of the Federation of Southern Women's Clubs. She organized the International Council of Women of the Darker Races of the World. She became chairperson of the Interracial Commission of Alabama. Washington was also present at the organizational meeting of the NACWC and later served as its fifth president from 1912 to 1916.

Another early leader in the Black women's movement was Agnes Jones Adams. A member of the Women's Era Club, she also served in the organization of the meetings and proceedings that resulted in the formation of the NACWC. At the organizing meeting, Adams served as one of the presiding officers. In later meetings, she continued as a speaker for the national agenda for the Association of Colored Women's Clubs.

These early leaders in the nineteenth century and early twentieth century were the pioneers for the advancement of African American women's clubs. This advancement took place not only in the increasing of the numbers of local and state clubs, but in the forward movement toward national unity. These were the women who performed the most difficult groundwork of beginning the winds of change by going against the prevailing direction. They were students, teachers, abolitionists, writers, organizers, and leaders. They were fearless in a fearful endeavor. For women to be uniting in America to assert their rights and status was out of the mainstream. For African American women to be uniting in America to assert their rights and status was far, far out of the mainstream. The intelligence and perseverance these women incorporated in doing what they did lead in the long run to the rise in personal/social status not only of themselves but for the masses.

History indicates the conditions that prevailed during the years after the Civil War. The dominant culture was not enthralled with emancipation and still considered African Americans an inferior race to the White population. Aside from the general daily discrimination by individuals, so-called Jim Crow laws were applied to keep the races separate not only on train cars and buses, but across the board in any public situation or accommodation. States passed laws against African Americans and laws that called for separation of the races. Indeed, a famous landmark federal court case was passed in 1895, *Plessy v. Ferguson*, which asserted that separate was equal. Oppression pervaded American society. The sum of the situation in American society caused a trend for organization to develop among African Americans to deal with the racial pressures put upon them. In 1890, T. Thomas Fortune, editor of the *New York Age*, declared that African Americans must take hold of the problem themselves and address it so loudly that the world will realize the oppression and attempt to right the wrong (Wesely, 1984, pp. 24–25). Fortune set up a meeting, which became known as the first organization for civic/political rights for African Americans. This organization, first named the Colored National League, became better known as the African American Council. Delegates from 23 states numbering over 120 individuals met in Chicago in 1890. A second meeting was held in 1891 in Nashville, but by 1893, Fortune had to realize the organization was financially bankrupt and was without widespread support. In subsequent years, it was revived at times, but though it faded from the picture, it provided its purpose. Local organizations began to flourish to discuss, decide, and act on issues of civic/political importance to African Americans. T. Thomas Fortune had played his part and would continue to do so.

Other organizations of note were begun as well. In 1892, Booker T. Washington began the Tuskegee Conferences. The goals were to help Blacks attain success in their industrial, educational, moral, and religious lives. Washington would stay close to the development of Black women's clubs and attempted to deliver his ideas, especially on industrial education, as planks in the NACWC's platform. Also, in 1896 the National Association of Colored Men was formed in Detroit. The goal of this group was to oppose the Tuskegee Conferences as being too accommodating to the dominant culture. This was the main argument against Washington at the time. Some groups thought Washington was too accommodating to Whites. These groups wanted the immediate granting of full rights, including citizenship. They did not want to wait for rights while footholds in the economy were established (see end of chapter: Washington and Du Bois). As with African American men, African American women took different sides of this issue.

As stated above, women had been organizing clubs on local levels and statewide in order to address local and state concerns. One of the earliest organizations was the Colored Women's League. This club was organized in the Washington, DC, area in 1892. The president was Helen Cook. In 1894, the Colored Women's League incorporated. Along with Cook, one of the members of the board to incorporate was Mary Church Terrell. The main stated goals of the club were to foster moral, intellectual, and social growth. The unstated goals were to drive for women's suffrage and equal rights. As always, the emphasis was on education to accomplish these goals. Night schools and kindergarten classes were established. An industrial committee was established to create programs in sewing, cooking, and gardening. All of these educational issues would become mainstays and more would be added. In addition, according to a Livingston County (Missouri) Library document entitled Bicentennial Memories of Negroes, it can be pointed out that as early as in 1893, Mary Church Terrell in an article in the *Afro-American Journal of Fashion* declared that the goal of the Colored Women's League was to bind together local clubs in a national organization (Williams, 1976).

Another key organization in the development of the birth of the NACWC was the Women's New Era Club of Boston. There were three leaders responsible for the establishment and leadership of this club. They were Josephine St. Pierre Ruffin, Florida Ruffin, and Maria Baldwin. The Women's New Era Club's purpose was to seek gifts of endowments with which kindergartens could be established. The group wanted to escalate the beginning of kindergarten so that it could encourage other groups to press the need for action in establishing the beginning of education along with education for mothers. Not only were those gifts obtained and kindergartens started in the Boston area, but gifts were attained in other areas that resulted in the establishment of kindergarten programs. One area of major success, for example, was the state of Georgia which developed multiple kindergartens in many areas of the state. In addition, working from her position as president of the Women's New Era Club, Josephine St. Pierre Ruffin is credited with publishing and editing the first newspaper by an African American woman, *Woman's Era*. Actually an illustrated magazine, it was said to have accomplished more for the national club idea than any other source (Wesely, 1984, p. 26).

There were so many local clubs forming around the country that it was inevitable that locals began to think about and consider a national organization. They were already communicating with each other by word of mouth and letter. State organizations were forming and they themselves held conventions. It was nothing new to have people from several states at a state conference. These people would go back home to share ideas they had learned and to tell others what clubs were doing and what issues they were emphasizing. In addition, local and state organizations were putting out their own newsletters that were being shared as widely as possible. Furthermore, while all of this was going on, all African Americans, but in particular women, were aware that the Sorosis Club of New York had created a national organization of White women's clubs in 1892. African Americans took notice of this immediately and began to realize that they would have to follow. It was now time for someone to take the lead and call for a national conference of African American women's clubs. This leadership came from Josephine St. Pierre Ruffin via the *Woman's Era* magazine of the Woman's New Era Club. Ruffin called the first national conference of colored women to Boston for July 29–31, 1895. The convention was originally named the First Congress of Colored Women, but when it actually took place, it was renamed the National Federation of African American Women (Wesely, 1984).

There were a couple of unique events in particular that spurred reasons for this first national meeting to be called. One came from what had to be one of the most action-inspiring editorials ever written. A man by the name of James W. Jacks, who was president of the Missouri Press Association, published an article attacking colored women as "wholly devoid of morality and that they were prostitutes, thieves, and liars" (Wesely, 1984, p. 28). After decades of attempting to concentrate on educational, social, and especially moral uplifting, this was an attack that stung the women deeply and caused for action to be taken. Jacks had sent his article to the secretary of the Anti-Slave Society of New England, Florence Belgarnie. Belgarnie, indignant with Jacks's accusations, passed it on to the editors of the *Woman's Era* suggesting they publish the article in order to stir outrage at its accusations, which would lead to action against Jacks and increased awareness of women's issues throughout the nation. Increased awareness, it was thought, would lead to increased public outcry for better conditions for women. When the editors received the article and the letter Jacks had written, they deliberated before taking action. The two Ruffins and Maria Baldwin were unsure of the effects of republishing the article Jacks had written. They understood the reaction of outrage that would come from African Americans. They believed most but not all African Americans would rise up against Jacks's accusations. They also felt that some African Americans as well as the majority of Whites would accept the article as fact. What was decided in the end was that the article would not be republished in fear of having people accept the content as true. Rather, in June of 1895, the editors chose in its magazine to describe carefully the article's contents in a review form. As expected, the description of Jacks's article riled people throughout the ranks who resented the accusations made by Jacks. The editors in response to the membership outcry sent copies of Jack's letter to Belgarnie to clubs across the country. The copy of the letter from Jacks was accompanied by a letter from Josephine St. Pierre Ruffin. Not only did this accompanying letter respond to Jacks, it called for a historic event that would be pivotal in the formation of the National Association of Colored Women's Clubs. On June 1, 1895, Josephine St. Pierre Ruffin, President of the Women's New Era Club of Boston, issued a call for a convention to take place July 29–31, 1895 (Wesely, 1984).

In addition to the rousing incident of Jacks's letter, there was another more subtle but equally effective set of circumstances that gave escalated impetus to a national conference of African American women and the birth of the NACWC. As a traveling elocutionist, Hallie Quinn Brown had been journeying around the country (and in England) delivering speeches regarding equal rights, and especially citizenship and voting rights, for African American women. As she traveled about, she noticed that in nearly every place she went women were seeking her out to explain the need for more connections between and among African American women who were working for the rights of women. They saw Brown as an excellent example of coordinating people of similar thinking as she shared information from town to town. However, they expressed that she as one person was not enough and that she did not stay anywhere very long. The women did not feel that enough information was being shared in her visits. They also felt that there was not enough detail in what she was sharing and no plan for coordination of continued work with others. Enough women along her tour impressed upon her the need for closer relationships of women in order to be more productive in accomplishing the goals the women had for their local and state groups that she decided to think about it and do something about the concern. Brown decided to meet with the Washington, DC, based Colored Women's League to share what she had learned and to press for a national association. This meeting and Brown's influence with the members of the active and influential Colored Women's League fed into the stir of Jacks's letter and increased the motivation and desire to begin thinking about a national organization.

Thus, the call had gone out and clubs in various locations were ready to answer the call—and answer they did. A committee was formed, led by Josephine St. Pierre Ruffin, to plan the organizational meeting, which assembled at Berkeley Hall, Boston, July 29–31, 1895. There were delegates from 10 states in attendance and representatives from 20 clubs. There were also individual women from 16 states and the District of Columbia who were there as independent yet interested people. Indeed the call had gone out, and indeed it had been answered. The people in attendance understood the personal/social status of African American women in America and the oppression and discrimination that accompanied it. They had now joined together in a larger, more organized fashion than ever before to advance the causes of women's clubs. The program reflected the interest in the familiar issues of local and state clubs. In addition to the need for national organization, the following issues can be found in the original program:

- Industrial training for women
- Higher education enrollment and graduation for women
- Pleas for social/civic/moral justice
- Race literature
- Political equality
- Social purity
- Temperance
- Suffrage
- Citizenship (Wesely, 1984, pp. 32–33)

Both women and men addressed the convention on these and other issues. Some of the notable speakers included Josephine St. Pierre Ruffin (acting as president or presider at this organizational meeting), Helen Cook, Margaret Murray Washington, Victoria Earle Mathews, T. Thomas Fortune, Henry Blackwell, and William Lloyd Garrison. Ruffin gave the welcome and keynote speech of the conference. In it, she celebrated the willingness and ability of African American women to do their part for the good of the people. On the second day of the meeting, Agnes Jones Adams gave an intriguing speech regarding social purity. This speech made a direct reference to the article Jacks had written and to the accusations he had made. On the third day of the meeting, the Committee on Resolutions, chaired by Ida Bell Wells Barnett, advocated equality for all Black workers. High priority was also placed on homemaking and home purchasing and the establishment of industrial schools. Mothers' meetings were proposed. An argument was presented against the withdrawal of federal troops in the South by President Hayes, which had resulted in the increased mistreatment of African Americans. Heavy criticism of separate coach cars in Louisiana was addressed. The committee expressed a desire to have both political parties condemn the practice of lynching as only the Republicans had done so (Wesely, 1984, pp. 32–34).

Within the recommendations of the Committee on Resolutions, it is easy to see the influence of the prevailing social thought and philosophy within the Black community at the time. The recognized leader of African Americans at this point in time was Booker T. Washington. His emphasis on industrial training to join the workforce of the industrial revolution coincided with the women's clubs' quest for the higher education of women, though not exactly. It also coincided with the urge of education for children, though Washington's ideas were seen as limited. Washington also strongly believed in homemaking and home purchasing as a way to earn respect, be productive, and make a way into the economy. His main philosophy was to get African Americans working in the economy of the industrial revolution in order to lift themselves up financially. These were the first steps, he thought, to other rights and freedoms which would come later. As previously mentioned, there were two camps (discussed further later in this chapter) on this issue not only in African American culture in general, but also among African American women. Some wanted a push for immediacy of all rights. Some were willing to wait as Washington was. At a time during which women were attempting to gain power and influence, it is intriguing to observe how Booker T. Washington, the most powerful and influential African American of the time, monitors this group and influences its ideas and work. It is equally intriguing to observe how Washington's main adversary and future successor, W.E.B. Du

Bois, manages his way into the women's club groups and the NACWC in order to influence its ideas and work. It seems that the influence of both of these leaders, though necessary, did not bowl over the members of women's clubs to the extent that they lost their own identity and agenda. They were split on the men's two different philosophies but united, for the most part, on the main issues of the NACWC. This, it would seem, is a marvelous tribute to the dedication to cause and commitment to action that the women's groups possessed. Not being usurped by the tremendous power, especially of Washington, indicates the power that they themselves had earned through the hard work, organization, and righteousness of their cause. Booker T. Washington was at this first organizational meeting and would continue to attend biennial meetings. Though his speech at this organizational meeting in July of 1895 is not itemized, it is known that in September of 1895 he made his famous speech at the Atlanta Cotton States and International Exposition regarding accommodating the needed industrial workforce while waiting for personal/social freedoms (Johnson, 2002, p. 133). In addition, Washington arranged for a second conference to take place in December of 1895 in Atlanta. Called the Atlanta Conference of Colored Women, at this conference Washington reiterated his demands for African Americans that he had made in September stating that "To earn a dollar in the factory just now is worth infinitely more than the opportunity to spend a dollar in the opera house" (Wesely, 1984, p. 35). Wesely reports that Washington's philosophy seemed to go unnoticed by this conference of women (p. 36). It is relevant to note that at the 1895 organizational meeting Margaret Murray Washington, Booker's wife, gave a speech, entitled *Individual Work for Mental Elevation*.

This first national meeting of African American women, called the National Federation of African American Women (often referred to as the National Federation of Afro-American Women), elected Josephine St. Pierre Ruffin as its first president on the first day of the meeting. Also elected as officers were Helen Cook and Margaret Murray Washington as vice-presidents and Eliza Carter as secretary. It would seem that carrying her presidency from the Women's New Era Club and her work in making the call into her role as president at the National Federation of African American Women at this meeting would be logical for Ruffin and this group. She, after all, did the most to this point to get the momentum going. She is listed in the original program as president, and accounts of the meeting indicate she was directing the meeting. On its third day, however, Margaret Murray Washington was elected as president (Wesely, 1984).

In 1896, the two best known established organizations for African American women met in Washington, DC, in back-to-back weeks. The Colored Women's League convention with Helen Cook as president met first. The many speakers at this convention included Fannie Jackson Coppin, Anna H. Jones, and Josephine Silone Yates. The speeches given were on the following topics:

- Establishment of kindergartens
- Industrial training for women
- Higher education for women
- Morality
- Careers for women
- Suffrage
- Citizenship (Wesely, 1984, p. 36)

Several individual speeches were given on different careers such as nursing, teaching, writing, and business. These had become issues of prime importance and in fact addressed the issues that had been long at the forefront of the advancement of personal/social status for African American women. To get a foothold in the professions would establish a foothold in society.

During the week following the Colored Women's League convention, the Federation of African American Women met. President Margaret Murray Washington greeted the audience in attendance and gave the keynote speech. Among the other many speakers at this conference were Helen Pitts Douglass (widow of Frederick Douglass) and Fannie Jackson Coppin. Main topics of discussion included prison reform, industrial training for women, and the elevation and improvement of domestic training, including motherhood and kindergarten (Wesely, 1984, pp. 36–38). At this convention, another historic event took place which would lead to the formation of the NACWC. A joint committee consisting of members of the Colored Women's League and the Federation of African American Women was created. This committee elected Mary Church Terrell as chair of the committee. It was this committee that made the resolution to join the two women's groups into one organization. The organization would be called the National Association of Colored Women. The resolution was put to the convention delegates for a vote. The resolution passed, the name was adopted, and after a full day of casting and recasting ballots, Mary Church Terrell was elected president of the new national organization. To end this historic conference, a call went out for the first convention of the National Association of Colored Women for September 15–17, 1897. This organization is now known as the National Association of Colored Women's Clubs (Wesely, 1984, pp. 36–38).

After the 1896 convention closed, means for broadening the awareness of the organization were sought. It was decided that the *Woman's Era* magazine would be the official mouthpiece of the NACWC (later to be replaced by *National Notes*). This was thought to be the logical way to spread the word of women's issues as well as to broaden the interest and involvement in order to establish a solid foothold in American society. In the August/September, 1896, issue of *Woman's Era* an article appeared entitled *First Statement as President of the National Association of Colored Women*. In this article, Mary Church Terrell urged members "to be forgetful of the past, hopeful of the future, and work in the present with undaunted courage and untiring zeal" (Wesely, 1984, p. 40). Other *Woman's Era* article topics in 1896 in preparation for the 1897 First Annual Convention included:

- Political and economic issues of the presidential election of 1896
- Education
- Women's issues, including suffrage and citizenship
- Paul Laurence Dunbar as a first-rate poet in the United States
- Legislation for colored people
- Appeals for the abolishment of discrimination
- Disapproval of *Plessy v. Ferguson* (compared to the Dred Scott Decision and antebellum days)
- Announcement of a lecture to be given by Maria Baldwin to the Brooklyn Institute of Arts and Sciences (the first time this institute had given an invitation to speak for the annual address) (Wesely, 1984, pp. 40–41)

Other notable events of club women in 1896 included the establishment of an association to maintain the Frederick Douglass home. Douglass was high in stature to African American women because of his 1848 second to the motion to address women's right to vote and because of his lifelong work in the advancement of women's issues. History will show that the NACWC spent a tremendous amount of time, effort, and money in honoring Douglass throughout the years in appreciation for his role in uplifting the status of women. Another notable event was the establishment of a series of conferences under the leadership of W.E.B. Du Bois that resulted in the publication of the *Atlanta University Studies*. These publications were meant to espouse Du Bois's beliefs regarding his "talented tenth" and the betterment and uplifting of African Americans. Du Bois demanded immediacy of personal/social/civic rights for all Americans. This latter event, then, completes the inclusion of the two leading and competing African American males at this time and their differing, almost opposite, ideas into the women's movement. Both wanted to influence the NACWC to their way of thinking, and both spent considerable time attempting to win over the NACWC and its growing number of members.

The First Annual Convention of the NACWC was held in Nashville, Tennessee, on September 15–17, 1897. As many as 63 delegates from 26 clubs and many states attended. They were greeted by President Mary Church Terrell in her President's Speech, which concluded that the home is the main avenue for improvement and advancement of African Americans. The home meant family, relationships, child rearing, education, and jobs. Living morally was always defined in these ways as well as in affiliation with religion. The rest of the conference program featured discussion of the organization's constitution and goals and many speeches on popular topics. Some of the many speakers included Fannie J. Jackson, Lizzy Williams, and Susan Adams. The following were themes of the many speeches:

- The Frederick Douglass monument
- Convict lease systems
- Separate car laws
- High moral standards
- Needs for mothers' meetings
- Education
- Kindergarten
- Temperance
- Suffrage
- Citizenship (Wesely, 1984, pp. 42–43)

Mary Church Terrell was reelected as president. Francis Jackson Coppin, Josephine St. Pierre Ruffin, Francis Ellen Watkins Harper, Josephine Silone Yates, Sylvania Williams, Jennie Chase Williams, and Lucy Thurman were all elected as vice-presidents. Anna V. Thompkins and Alice Ruth Moore were elected secretaries. Mary Trisbee Handby was elected treasurer. Victoria Earle Mathews was elected as National Organizer. Margaret Murray Washington was elected as Chair of the Executive Board, and J. Napier Kemp was elected as chair of Ways and Means.

One important order of business was deciding on a constitution. In working through discussions for the NACWC constitution, many ideas were presented and, as would be expected, arguments over those ideas took place. Language was particularly controversial. Discussion included the use of the phrase "by the help of God" as an important qualifier of guardianship. The motion to use this phrase was made by Lucy Thurman, and the motion was passed and adopted as part of the constitution. The usual membership requirements, program procedures, and voting procedures were included in addition to what The African American Registry reports would eventually become the long-lasting goals of the organization. Seven national goals adopted by the NACWC were the following:

1. To promote the education of women and children
2. To raise the standards of the home
3. To improve conditions for family living
4. To work for the moral, economic, social, and religious welfare of women and children
5. To protect the rights of women and children
6. To secure and enforce civil and political rights for the African American race
7. To promote interracial understanding so that justice may prevail among all people (African American Registry, 2005, p. 1)

These goals essentially have survived the evolution of the organization and remain today, though stated in slightly altered verbiage and with some additions, as the objectives of the NACWC.

There was another order of business. The Resolutions Committee played an important and essential role at this first annual meeting. What resolutions would be passed would set the standards for future resolution committees and indeed the avenues of discussion important to delegates at future conferences. Five important resolutions adopted at the First Annual Convention of the NACWC were the following:

1. Clubs should petition state legislatures for the repeal of the separate car law.
2. The Tennessee Industrial School was to be petitioned to give colored boys an equal chance to attend to learn trades.
3. Endorsement of the establishment of the John Brown Industrial School, the Douglass Memorial Monument, and the establishment of homes for the aged and reformatories for delinquents should occur.

4. Opposition to juvenile secret societies, crime, liquor trafficking, and lynching should be announced.
5. Support and commendation for the Women's Christian Temperance Union should be made. (Wesely, 1984, p. 43)

The close of this historic First Annual Convention noted the location and date of the first biennial meeting to be Chicago in 1899. With the announcement of this First Annual Convention, clearly, the NACWC was showing its resiliency to the pitfalls of beginning a new organization. It had adopted a constitution, identified national goals, entertained affiliates from far and wide, elected officers, charted a future course, and set the location and date of its next meeting (Wesely, 1984, p. 45). All of this was accomplished in addition to the many speeches/presentations given that stimulated discussion of the very issues of most concern to club members. Indeed, it appeared that the National Association of Colored Women's Clubs was here to stay.

Having held the organizational meeting in 1896 and the First Annual Convention in 1897, the National Association of Colored Women's Clubs in 1899 held what was to become the First Biennial Meeting of the National Association of Colored Women's Clubs. Thus, a regular schedule (with limited alterations) of biennial meetings in different locations around the country has been in place since 1899 to the present. These meetings would continue the discussion of the national umbrella of issues related to local and state concern. In this way, the national association not only led the local and state club work via the national agenda, but listened to, took pride in, and supported the work of local and state clubs. A working relationship developed on all levels that led to a common philosophy and mission from which to gain civil rights and privileges as well as first-class citizenship for all. The NACWC motto, *Lifting as We Climb*, stands as a symbol for as the club women gain, they lift the status of all people, in particular Black people, especially Black women. The motto was adopted with the intention of showing "an ignorant and suspicious world that our aims and interests are identical with those of all good, aspiring women" (African American Registry, 2005). In commenting on the motto, Mary Church Terrell wrote the club's members "have determined to come in to the closest possible touch with the masses of our women, through whom the womanhood of our people is always judged" (Giddings, 1984, p. 98). Author Paula Giddings (1984) states in her writing of women's history that "For these Black women, character was judged by where a woman wanted to go rather than where she was" (p. 98).

The 1899 Biennial Meeting of the National Association of Colored Women's Clubs convened in Chicago on August 14–16. President Mary Church Terrell opened the meeting with her welcome and review of the unfolding of the establishment of the NACWC. The gist of her comments was an enthusiastic expression that individual local and even state clubs could accomplish little alone, but they could accomplish much with the support and organization of a national association with a national agenda and a following of various parties of interest. Great accomplishments, she stated, would be achieved through the togetherness and connection and common goals of the national organization in conjunction with local and state branches. Terrell's remarks were well received, and her enthusiasm was met with an equally enthusiastic response. Other opening remarks were made by several local business people who welcomed the delegates and representatives to Chicago. Booker T. Washington also addressed the opening of this conference. His welcome included, to be sure, his pitch for industrial education and the furthering of African American entry into the American industrial job market (Wesely, 1984, pp. 45–49).

The formal program consisted of the presentation of papers by many notable women including Josephine Silone Yates, Carrie Fortune, Lucy Thurman, and Elizabeth Carter. Terrell, herself, delivered three speeches: *Convention Welcome*, *The Progress of Colored Women*, and *The Life of Harriet Beecher Stowe*. Josephine Silone Yates delivered a speech entitled, *Social Necessity of an Equal Moral Standard for Men and Women*. Other speeches provided more thoughts on the familiar topics of concern for NACWC: child rearing, convict lease programs, labor questions, lynch laws, practical club work, kindergartens, equal moral standards for men and women, prison work, race literature, temperance reform, suffrage, and citizenship. One other presentation by Mary Church Terrell was printed and sold to delegates and representatives for ten cents each. This tactic was used so that people would not only have an interest in kindergarten, but they would have a plan from which to establish kindergarten. It also earned money for the club coffers. A speech by Josephine B. Bruce regarding the unequal treatment of Blacks and Whites by labor unions resulted in a resolution that demanded that labor unions stop their shortsighted and crude treatment of Blacks. A committee was formed to lobby union leaders for equal treatment. When it came time to elect a president for the next two years, several candidates vied for the position. Josephine B. Bruce, Margaret Murray Washington, Lucy Thurman, Josephine St. Pierre Ruffin, Mary Church Terrell, and Josephine Silone Yates all ran and received votes. The eagerness to serve was obvious. Mary Church Terrell was reelected for the 1899–1901 biennial (Wesely, 1984, pp. 45–49).

There were other events worth mentioning surrounding the First Biennial Meeting. W.E.B. Du Bois, in what seems to be more drama in the competition for influence with Booker T. Washington for a certain amount of ideological management of the NACWC, went out of his way during the meetings to publish overly flattering remarks. He was effusive in his praise for the intelligence, beauty, and culture of the women in attendance at the meeting. Also, Jane Addams of Hull House invited the delegates to a luncheon. The *Chicago Times Herald* reported that "This was the first time that colored women have been given the decided recognition in a social way by a woman of lighter skin" (Wesely, 1982, p. 48). This event was seen as progress.

This 1899 Biennial Meeting rooted the NACWC as a national organization of prominence that was firmly established in American society and would remain so into the future. The election of officers from several different states enhanced the status of the organization and added to its recognition as permanent. The importance of this firm foundation is manifold. It gives impetus to universal recognition of crucial issues of African American women. It gives motivation, coordination, and direction to local and state clubs that follow the goals of the national organization. Clubs now were able to see a national vision that was much larger than local or state issues but still connected. Local and state groups felt good about being part of a bigger picture. In addition to all these benefits, a permanent, popular, influential, successful national organization also makes other national groups and individuals of influence pay attention to its ideas and goals and desires. To this end in this case, the leading national women's group until this point in time, the General Federation of Women's Clubs, was so influenced by the success of the NACWC that it recognized the NACWC as a viable organization and needed to consider its agenda. Realizing that these two organizations had some common interests, the president of the state delegation of Georgia to the Fifth Biennial Convention of the General Federation of Women to be held in Milwaukee asked Josephine St. Pierre Ruffin to attend. However, when Ruffin agreed and registered, a problem developed. It was suggested that she register only as a member from a White club and not as a member of the Black Women's New Era Club. When Ruffin insisted upon being registered as a member of the Women's New Era Club, an argument ensued. Refusing to back down, Ruffin escalated her demands that not only she be accepted on the basis of her gender (not race), but that the Women's New Era Club be accepted on the basis of its business, not because of the race of its members. This insistence triggered a heated debate with resolutions in favor of and against Ruffin's demands. Northern delegates urgently requested that the federation drop race issues and allow the two demands. Southern delegates insisted on White-only language to be made even more clearly written into the constitution. Ballots went back and forth. In the end, Ruffin was not recognized as a delegate nor was the New Era Club recognized.

Reaction to the exclusion of Ruffin and the Women's New Era Club presented some interesting ideas. First, the exclusion of African Americans from the General Federation of Women inspired, renewed, and reinvigorated the efforts of the NACWC. This, by extension, redoubled the efforts of local and state clubs to work toward their goals. Second, this circumstance helped to diffuse the idea put forth by White people and resented by the African Americans that they wanted to keep separate from White people, to keep to their own. Clearly, Blacks wanted to join Whites in mutual work and progress, but Whites refused to cooperate. Finally, a related incident summarized the thoughts and feelings of African Americans regarding the refusal of their acceptance into the General Federation of Women. Before the convention, a Black women's club from Racine, Wisconsin, made application to attend the Fifth Biennial Convention of the General Federation of Women. The club was told that the application had been received too late. In response, R. H. Anderson, President of the Racine Phyllis Wheatley Club, stated "This is an old fight all over again. Years ago, the men in the South fought our men. Now the women are fighting us" (Wesely, 1982, p. 50). A year later, in 1900, the General Federation of Women changed its constitution to allow African American women full rights as delegates. Ruffin had taken a stand that caused change and made a difference in the progress of African American women, all women, all people.

Progress then. Progress now. The National Association of Colored Women's Clubs began in 1896 as a method to make a difference. By 1900, that difference was being seen. For the next 117 years more barriers would fall, more opportunities would be developed, and more people of all colors would benefit. Enough? No. However, without the National Association of Colored Women's Clubs where would we be now?

Washington and Du Bois

Booker T. Washington and W. E. B. Du Bois would not be considered lesser-known Black heroes. They are well known in history and studied substantially in American schools and universities. Indeed, they should not be considered as stories for the purposes of maintaining the theme of this book and thus should be looked upon more as national leaders rather than local heroes. Nevertheless, because of the important roles they played in contributing to the goals and actions of the National Association of Colored Women's Clubs (NACWC) and because they both courted and wooed favor with the NACWC, some mention should be made of their work and their basic ideas. In this sense, what is shared here is meant to enhance the chapter and to increase understanding in creating connections between the NACWC, these two particular national leaders, and the work of local people in relation to opposing perspectives. The brief description below reveals further the strong appeal and potential power that the NACWC wielded as it grew in numbers and stature. For these two influential and powerful people to be competing for approval by the NACWC indicates, in the end, the very success of the National Association of Colored Women's Clubs.

A turning point in the development of American educational history and, most likely, equal rights for African Americans, occurred in 1895 when Booker T. Washington gave his famous speech at the opening of the Cotton States and International Exposition in Atlanta, Georgia. This brilliantly worded address, often referred to as the Southern Compromise, has been a topic of interest to scholars as it has been discussed as either the beginning of the end of segregated school ideas in America or as another setback in desegregation efforts. Some have interpreted the speech as a 50-year setback to desegregation as followers of Washington redoubled their efforts at opening segregated schools; however, as W.E.B. Du Bois entered the debate in opposition to Washington, others believed Du Bois had more impact on the development of educational and social equality in the decades immediately following Washington's speech as he escalated the criticism of Washington's ideas and pushed for full equality. Du Bois demanded immediacy in the achievement of full Constitutional rights for African Americans in opposition to Washington's idea of gradualism, which accepted a much slower achievement of full equality while establishing a useful education for African Americans. The question becomes whose technique (stance) was more effective, appropriate, or desired in the attempt to establish both educational and social rights. There is no definitive answer to this question.

With the African American desire for educational opportunity offset by the dominant culture's desire for discrimination and segregation, an uneasy system of segregated education accompanied America's entrance into the industrial age. Moving from an agrarian society to an industrial society created a new set of circumstances for the purposes of public schools. To accommodate the numbers of workers needed in new American factories, schools were called on to create and deliver industrial education, which would, in turn, create and deliver a newly skilled work force for the new American economy. In the North, powerful industrialists were demanding a qualified work force for their factories. In the South, would-be industrialists promoted industrial education for African Americans. By the 1890s, African Americans both in the North and the South had long since concluded that the struggle for and the eventual attainment of educational opportunities would also improve economic, political, and social conditions. The link between educational rights and political/social (civil) rights had been made first via the struggle for educational opportunity and then via the struggle for equal educational opportunity. With the passing of the 1895 *Plessy v. Ferguson* Supreme Court case and its subsequent upholding in 1896, the battle was only half won. There would be educational opportunity, especially for industrial education, but separate would be called equal even though everyone knew it wasn't. Advances in social equality were slow to nil.

The answer to the question of education for African Americans came in a speech made by African American leader Booker T. Washington in Atlanta, Georgia, in September of 1895. Washington was a Southern Black who had been born into slavery and educated at Hampton Institute in Virginia. Hampton promoted the education of freed slaves to become teachers of proper work habits for other freed slaves. It was a school at which long, hard, manual work was seen as *the dignity of labor* (Spring, 2011, p. 222) supposedly preparing African Americans to enter the dominant culture and reap the fruits of its economic advantage while eventually leading to political/social rights down the road. Washington's time at Hampton encouraged him to use it as a model for Tuskegee Normal and Industrial Institute, which he developed in Alabama in 1881. The Tuskegee idea was to provide practical education for African Americans so that they could find jobs in the marketplace. In the years since 1881, Washington had been writing and speaking, both to Black and White audiences, about the education of African Americans from the Tuskegee point of view. An example can be seen in his 1885 article entitled *The Educational Outlook in the South* in which he states "Brains, property, and character for the Negro will settle the question of civil right" (Johnson, 2002, p. 130). Later in the same article he states "…any work looking towards the improvement of the Negro south, must have for one of its aims…to live… with his white neighbors both socially and politically" (Johnson, 2002,

p. 131). This second passage, especially, seems to establish Washington's clear notion that education for employment is the pathway to political and social, and thus civil, equality. To further solidify his point of industrial education for African Americans as the essential ingredient, Washington, in his book *Up from Slavery*, discounts such traditional education as French grammar or other "book learning" as a waste of time in building the proper work habits for advancement (Washington, 1963, pp. XIII–XIV). It is in this context that Washington delivers his speech in 1895.

The loudest response to Booker T. Washington's ideas came from W. E.B. Du Bois, a Northern free Black who was educated at Fisk University, Harvard University, and the University of Berlin. A Ph. D. and a leading American sociologist, he was an early leader in the struggles for civil rights for African Americans. Du Bois founded the National Association for the Advancement of Colored People in 1909 and was editor of the magazine *Crises*. In his book, *The Souls of Black Folk: Essays and Sketches*, he attacks Washington's ideas. Du Bois begins his criticism by stating that Washington is only interested in work and money and that Washington completely ignores "the higher aims of life" (Du Bois, 1961, pp. 36–42). Du Bois sees Washington as pushing submission to the White man at a time, after the war, when what was needed was not submission, but rather, an intensification of the assertion of citizenship rights. He asserts that acquiring education only to buy material possessions is not enough and creates indignity. Du Bois calls Washington old fashioned in his attempt to appease and to submit to the dominant culture. He is outraged at Washington's willingness to give in at a time when acceleration in human rights should take place. Du Bois claims that Washington is asking African Americans to give up political power, insistence on civil rights, and the higher education of youth in order to "concentrate all their energies on industrial education, the accumulation of wealth, and the conciliation of the South" (Johnson, 2002, p. 137). Du Bois sees this focus as superficial and conciliatory. Thus, he concludes that Washington's Southern Compromise ended in a disaster for Black people, especially in the South. Du Bois asserts that Washington has accepted and is promoting the inferior status of Negroes. Du Bois wanted a different education for African Americans. He wanted to protect the political and social rights of African Americans, and he wanted African American leaders in both the North and the South to promote this type of education rather than an industrial education to provide for a dominant culture work force. He believed that all African Americans should be involved in a constant struggle to obtain equal rights as granted all citizens in the American Constitution and that educational systems should reflect, represent, and strive for this. He wanted African Americans never to give up the struggle and never to compromise the struggle but to push on constantly, unwaveringly, ever diligent in the struggle for equal rights in every aspect of the name. He sought immediacy as Washington sought gradualism.

In the end, it can be said without question that both Washington and Du Bois had the same long-term goals for educational equality and civil rights even though they espoused two different plans to achieve them. Washington believed that Blacks had to start at the bottom of the work force and gradually work their way up to positions of leadership and responsibility as a path to equal citizenship. He accepted a temporary position of inferiority for Blacks. Du Bois wanted Blacks to immediately have the same rights guaranteed Whites in the Constitution. He would not accept a temporary position of inferiority for Blacks. Clearly, each man was striving for equality for his people in all aspects of American life and citizenry. No one can doubt the sincerity of each in his attempts to plot out the best course for his people and then to lead Blacks and Whites alike into believing this was indeed the best plan. Washington may be praiseworthy for his bold attempts to get education for employment while he deemphasized political, social, and civil rights in a plan to eventually arrive at civil rights across all elements of American society. By the same token, Washington may be criticized for his lack of all-encompassing civil rights advocacy in his Atlanta Cotton States and International Exposition speech, which seemed to result in the promotion and escalation of the use of segregated schools. Washington's idea was clear. He spent the better part of 35 years attempting to establish the notion of gradualism and accommodation in his quest for equality. Du Bois, however, diametrically opposed Washington's ideas in an effort to promote immediate equality throughout political, social, and educational arenas. The question becomes whose technique of ultimately gaining these rights was more effective and appropriate for the time. History reports that Washington's ideas won acceptance during his lifetime. After his death in 1915, his leadership and ideas were passed over in favor of the more militant views of Du Bois. Du Bois would not submit to any compromise of rights or conciliatory accommodation. He always pressed for immediacy. Had his ideas come to prominence sooner than they did, might they have resulted in more or faster political, social, and educational equality than Washington's ideas? Would this refusal to compromise have resulted in an entirely different experience for African Americans (and thus, for all Americans)? Was Du Bois, in the long run, more responsible than Washington in the passing of civil rights legislation and the success of the civil rights movement? The answers to these questions for every individual lie in the personal assessment and analysis of the many and varied factors that interplay in the complexity of the very questions themselves and the plethora of personal, emotional, social, and intellectual elements therein. Washington and Du Bois were two inspirational thinkers who led the way for the transition of American culture.

Glossary

African American Registry: A nonprofit organization offering educational resources for Black history and heritage.

Atlanta (Southern) Compromise: An 1895 speech by Booker T. Washington that offered an agreement with Southern White leaders for the employment of African Americans in the industrial economy.

Atlanta University Studies: A series of studies edited by W.E.B. Du Bois that represent systematic social science inquiry into the conditions and lives of African Americans.

Chicago Times Herald: A nineteenth century newspaper established in Chicago, Illinois, formed from a merger between the *Chicago Times* and the *Chicago Herald* and which favored and supported republican policies.

Elocutionist: A person's manner of speaking in public based on the study and practice of oral delivery, including control of both voice and gesture.

Federation of Women's Clubs: This club, formed at a conference in New York in 1889, included 3000 women from 61 women's clubs and was modeled after the Sorosis Club of New York.

Icon: A person or object regarded as a symbol or representative of something that is revered or idolized.

Lifting as We Climb: Josephine St. Pierre Ruffin is said to be the originator of this National Association of Colored Women's Club motto that desired to show a positive image of African Americans.

National Association of Colored Women's Clubs: Formed in 1896 from several individual women's clubs, its purpose was to demonstrate to an "ignorant and suspicious world that women's aims and interests are identical with those of all good and aspiring women."

National Notes: This journal replaced *Woman's Era* magazine as the official journal of the National Association of Colored Women's Clubs.

National Women's Suffrage Association: Formed in 1896 in New York City by Susan B. Anthony and Elizabeth Cady Stanton to oppose the 15th Amendment unless it included women's right to vote.

New York Age: One of the most influential African American newspapers of its time, 1887–1953, its roots included the 1880 *New York Freeman Newspaper* cofounded by T. Thomas fortune.

North Star: This famous African American newspaper was published by Frederick Douglass who created the *North Star* motto, which in part stated that right is of no sex and truth is of no color.

Universal Suffrage: The right to vote not restricted by race, sex, belief, wealth, or social status.

Women's Era: This well-known newspaper/journal/magazine was the voice of the women's movement during its time, 1894–1897, and was founded by Josephine St. Pierre Ruffin and Florida R. Ridley.

Women's New Era Club: This club established in 1893 by Josephine St. Pierre Ruffin, Florida Ruffin, and Maria Baldwin in Boston, first sought funding to establish kindergartens and then broadened its scope to include women's issues and concerns, which mirrored and sustained the growing agenda of the women's movement of the time.

Discussion/Reflection

1. This chapter attempts to convince us that White women and Black women worked together toward mutual progress. Do you agree that this happened? How do you analyze the relationship between White women and Black women in this chapter?
2. Which clubs, societies, magazines, journals, newspapers, groups, or other such associations were you aware of before you read this chapter? How had you known about them before? List and briefly describe a few of these from the chapter.
3. The chapter identifies many individuals both well known and not so well known. Which of the people in this chapter had you heard of before? How had you known about them? Briefly discuss two people in this chapter by writing of their significance.
4. Choose an individual from this chapter that stood out to you, perhaps more so than all the rest. Explain the reasons this person stood out to you among the many people of the chapter.
5. No matter what gender you are how does this chapter relate to you personally? Have you experienced any of what the people in the chapter have experienced and have you felt as any of the people in the chapter have felt? Explain.
6. What do you think motivated James W. Jacks to say what he said about African American women?
7. When you look at the issues listed in the original program for the meeting in Boston in 1895, what issues do you think have been solved by today and what issues still need attention in contemporary society? In other words, what has been the progress so far?

8. When you review the topics of the speeches given at the 1896–1897 conventions, which topics stand out to you? Why do they stand out? What do the topics tell you about society near the end of the nineteenth century?
9. Comment on the seven national goals adopted by the NACWC. Would you drop any? Would you add any? Do you understand their purposes?
10. Describe the state of gender equality in American society today. What progress has been made? What are the continuing or new issues? Be sure to be specific in your explanations and support of your description.

Selected Topics for Further Study

1. Women's Rights Convention, Seneca Falls, 1948
2. Sojourner Truth, Elizabeth Cady Stanton, William Wells Brown, Charles Lenox Remond, Frederick Douglas
3. *North Star* newspaper
4. National Association of Colored Women's Clubs
5. National Women's Suffrage Association
6. Sorosis Club
7. Federation of Women's Clubs
8. *Woman's Era* magazine/*Woman's Era* newspaper
9. T. Thomas Fortune
10. Booker T. Washington
11. The Tuskegee Conferences
12. National Association of Colored Men
13. *African American Journal of Fashion*
14. James W. Jacks
15. Florence Belgarnie
16. Higher education of African American women and men
17. President Hayes
18. African Americans and the industrial revolution
19. W.E.B. Du Bois
20. Women's clubs today

References

African American Registry (2005). National Association of Women's Clubs formed! Retrieved from http://www.aaregistry.org/historic_events/view/national-association-colored-womens-clubs-formed

Demos, J. (1970). *A little commonwealth: Family life in Plymouth colony.* New York: Oxford University Press.

Du Bois, W. E. B. (1961). *The Souls of Black folk: Essays and sketches.* Greenwich: Fawcett.

Giddings, P. (1984). *When and where I enter: The impact of Black women on race and sex in America.* New York: Perennial.

Johnson, T. W. (2002). *Historical documents in American education.* Boston: Allyn & Bacon.

Spring, J. (2011). *The American school: A global context from the Puritans to the Obama era* (8th ed.). New York: McGraw-Hill.

Washington, Booker T. (1963). *Up from slavery.* Garden City, New Jersey: Doubleday.

Wesely, C. H. (1984). *The history of the National Association of Colored Women's Clubs, Inc.: A legacy of service.* Washington, DC: National Association of Colored Women's Clubs.

Williams, L. E. (1976). Bicentennial memories of negroes. Livingston County Library. Retrieved from http://www.livingstoncountylibrary.org/History/People/negroes.htm

· 4 ·

UNCOVERING EZEKIEL GILLESPIE

African American Male Suffrage

"White citizens of the United States, foreign residents who intended to become citizens, and certain Indians"
—Voting proposal for Wisconsin State Constitution, 1846

Ezekiel Gillespie is not a well-known figure in African American history. His story remains largely untold. Though his contributions mainly took place in the state of Wisconsin, it could be said that the impact of what he did in Wisconsin contributed to the African American right of suffrage throughout the United States. Whether or not his story is known, Ezekiel Gillespie made a difference. This chapter attempts to uncover Ezekiel Gillespie as a significant contributor to African American history and seeks to preserve his name and his contributions. Ezekiel Gillespie's story needs to be told for at a time of no voting power for Blacks in a racist society it was he who proffered the notion of a legal voting system.

As Wisconsin was preparing to become a state in 1848, two conventions were held. The first convention, sometimes referred to as the Statehood Convention, was held in 1846. The second convention, usually referred to as the Constitutional Convention, was held in 1847–1848. Both conventions meant to establish the state of Wisconsin and provide an abiding constitution. They both also addressed the issue of Black suffrage. In 1846, the Suffrage Committee of the convention created and proposed an article for the Wisconsin State Constitution that allowed "white citizens of the United States, foreign residents who intended to become citizens, and certain Indians" to be allowed to vote (Harper, 2003). Recognizing that African Americans were not included in this article, a separate, stand-alone article was written to include African American suffrage. As parts of a constitutional proposal that was defeated, neither of these articles was allowed to become law. That the second article did pursue Black suffrage indicated there was an interest in pursuing this civil right. That is to say that though Black suffrage was left out of the constitution, early indications were that there was an interest in the issue and its passage. It may be significant that in that vote 34% of the delegates voted in favor of the article regarding Black suffrage (Harper, 2003). At the 1847–1848 convention, delegates included and ratified language granting the right to vote to "white male persons, over the age of twenty-one years, who have resided in this state one year next preceding any election, and who are citizens of the United States or who have declared their intentions to become citizens, and also certain persons of Indian blood" (Williams, 2005). This language again excluded certain populations, including African Americans; however, a stipulation was attached to the language that permitted the legislature to extend suffrage to those persons not included. This stipulation seems to increase the amount of interest in Black suffrage. However, there was a qualifier. The qualifier was that the constitution required a referendum vote for approval by "a majority of all the votes cast at such an election" (Ranney, 1995, p. 4). So in order for suffrage to occur a referendum had to be called. This was clearly in opposition to the rights granted or inferred in the constitution.

It happened that the first state legislature passed a Black suffrage law and authorized a referendum in the form of a general election in November of 1849. In this general election, the law was approved by a vote of 5265–4075. However, because fewer than half of all votes went in favor of the Black suffrage issue, it was viewed that the law had failed (Ranney, 1997). In this general election, there were other issues to be decided, and there were also individuals vying for political offices. According to constitutional language, it was deemed that 5265 votes represented a number less than half of all votes cast in the general election and therefore the suffrage article was defeated. The courts and the citizens accepted this conclusion and African Americans were not allowed to begin voting. That is where it was left until 1857. Both in 1857 and in 1865 the Wisconsin legislation put forth new suffrage laws meant to legalize Black voting rights. These laws also failed to get enough votes in referendums. Although these two laws failed, it may be significant that compared to 1846 when 34% of delegates voted in favor of Black suffrage, the 1857 and 1865 percentages were 41% and 46% respectively (Harper, 2003). This would seem to indicate that the issue was growing in popularity toward eventual passage. Still, the failure of these two laws left African Americans unable to vote by the year 1865. So as the Civil War was ending and African Americans found themselves looking toward new beginnings, they were still denied the civil/equal right of suffrage.

Ezekiel Gillespie was said to have been born on or about May 31, 1818, in Greene County, Tennessee. The circumstances of his birth have never been substantiated but enough is known that some conclusions can be drawn. The name Gillespie was a prominent name in the Greene County area in 1818. Since then, families have grown to the point that both Blacks and Whites in the area are now known as Gillespies. In the beginning, however, four Scottish brothers came to the area and settled in the early 1700s. Of the four, one or perhaps two settled in Greene County. The others settled in nearby Washington County as well as in Virginia and North Carolina. By 1830 in Greene County, three Gillespie families were identified that had African American boys of the right approximate age to be Ezekiel. Because there were only a small number of free Blacks living in Greene County and none of them named Gillespie, the facts lead to the conclusion that Ezekiel Gillespie was a slave. Indeed, his obituary in the *Evening Wisconsin* newspaper claims that he bought his freedom from his father. Census information from 1850 to 1880 identifies Gillespie as a mulatto. The Wisconsin State Supreme Court stated that he was "half White and half African American blood." Ezekiel Gillespie appears to be the son of a Black woman and a slave owner (Holzhueter, 1977, p. 180).

Birth records do not reveal anything about the first two or three decades of Gillespie's life. It is known that when his first daughter was born in 1845 or 1846 he was living somewhere in Indiana. It is known that he was living in Evansville, Indiana, in 1849 (Holzhueter, 1977, p. 179). It is significant to understand that Evansville is a town right on the Ohio River and is well recognized as an Underground Railroad escape route. This knowledge and what is learned in the study of the rest of his life illuminate the general sense that Ezekiel Gillespie was engaged in civil rights issues throughout his life. He chose not to discuss his involvement with friends or family, but it can be seen both in Indiana and Wisconsin that he was clearly active in African American causes. Ezekiel Gillespie's second daughter was born sometime in the summer of 1849 in Evansville. His wife Sophia was born in North Carolina in about 1828.

By 1850, Gillespie was earning a living selling small goods and produce. He was an independent entrepreneur who may have sold his goods from a roadside stand or by going door-to-door. Probably because of the Fugitive Slave Act of 1850 and the resulting brutality toward African Americans, Gillespie moved to Wisconsin in 1852. He settled in Milwaukee and continued his trade of selling goods, mostly groceries and vegetables and chicken. It is important and interesting to note that Gillespie advertised his products in the *Milwaukee Free Democrat*, an abolitionist newspaper edited by Sherman Booth, a well-known and outspoken abolitionist and civil rights advocate (Holzhueter, 1977, p. 180).

The recession of 1857 was as difficult for Ezekiel Gillespie as it was for most other Americans. One would assume that Gillespie's business suffered a doomed fate in that year. Holzhueter (1977) reports that though his name does appear in the Milwaukee City Directory for 1857, there is no occupation listed. Indeed, in 1858 Gillespie's name doesn't appear in the directory at all. This would lead to the assumption that hard times were upon Ezekiel and that his business probably suffered or folded. Nothing more than that is known about him at this time. There appears, however, to be a comeback in 1859 as not only does Gillespie's name reappear in the directory, but he is listed as having a new job. This became the job of his life as he was able to associate himself with a well-known leader in Milwaukee. In 1859 Gillespie established himself as a porter for Alexander Mitchell, a wealthy and successful Milwaukee banking and railroad executive. Gillespie began his career with Mitchell working in the bank office as essentially a messenger. He later moved to the headquarters of the Chicago, Milwaukee, and St. Paul Railway Company. Mitchell was its president. Gillespie worked for the Chicago, Milwaukee, and St. Paul Railway Company for the rest of his life and was reported to be a respected employee. Even when the railway moved its headquarters to Chicago in 1890, Gillespie stayed with the company and moved to Chicago with it. He was working for the company when he died in 1892 (Holzhueter, 1977, p. 181).

Sophia preceded Ezekiel in death in 1864. In 1866, he married Catherine Robinson of Lima, Ohio. Catherine was a very religious person. She was a member of the African Methodist Episcopal Church in Lima. This affiliation and her devotion to religion probably led her to later influence Ezekiel to take part with her in establishing a church in Milwaukee. Catherine had two children from a previous marriage and by this time Ezekiel had five children from his marriage to Sophia. Together Catherine and Ezekiel produced four more children for a total of eleven children. In 1869, they established the first African Methodist Episcopal church in Milwaukee and in Wisconsin. Establishing this church with Catherine is considered Ezekiel's second big contribution to Wisconsin history. Catherine also preceded Ezekiel in death, passing away in 1874 (Holzhueter, 1977, p. 183).

Though one can really only speculate on Gillespie's civil rights involvement prior to 1865, evidence does exist to show that he was involved in Black suffrage beginning in 1865 and onward. In the year 1865, several petitions were being passed around to attempt to initiate legislation regarding Black suffrage. Ezekiel was not only a signer of one of these petitions, but he was one of seven men (Milwaukee Seven) who called a meeting in Milwaukee to further the advancement of suffrage (Holzhueter, 1977, p. 182). The seven men met to establish ways and methods of stirring the public interest to rally the public enough to force legislators to put forth a referendum. On their personal/local level, they were planning action to make a difference. While the Milwaukee Seven met, the *Evening Wisconsin* newspaper began to advocate a court case regarding the suffrage issue (Holzhueter, 1977). There is no evidence that these two events were working in tandem. History does not seem to reveal so. The seven-man committee from Milwaukee appeared to be citizen leaders who were meeting regarding a local but important issue based on their personal desires. The newspaper's strategy was meant to convince the Wisconsin State Supreme Court that suffrage was already in place and legal because of the 1849 referendum. It was taking the chance that the court would reconsider the earlier assumption of failure to pass because of a lack of majority of votes cast. As the Milwaukee Seven believed it could convince the general public to force Black suffrage by pressing legislators, the newspaper believed it could convince the court to now conclude that the language of the law, "a majority of all votes cast at an election," meant a majority of votes cast on a single, specific issue, which in this case was Black suffrage. So while the Milwaukee Seven pushed the general public to persuade legislators to once again establish a referendum, the *Evening Wisconsin* created a plan of action to bring the issue to the Supreme Court.

This brings us back to Sherman Booth. It is known that Booth had owned a newspaper prior to 1865 and had sold that newspaper to the *Evening Wisconsin*. Booth, then, knew the owner of the *Evening Wisconsin*, and it can be assumed he had a relationship with its owner and editors. In fact, a story in the *Evening Wisconsin* 32 years later identifies Booth as the person who was involved with Gillespie in the actual unfolding of events found in the court case (Holzhueter, 1977). This not only links Gillespie to Sherman Booth but by extension (because of Booth's involvement in abolitionist causes) to Underground Railroad activity in both Indiana and Wisconsin. When Byron Paine is added as Gillespie's lawyer in the court case, Ezekiel Gillespie's involvement in civil rights issues is solidified beyond a reasonable doubt. At the time, Paine was the most popular and well-known civil rights lawyer. Paine had in fact represented Booth himself in the famous Glover case of 1854 in Milwaukee (Boers, 2008). That Booth and Paine would be so involved with Gillespie is further evidence that suggests he was involved in civil rights issues before, during, and most likely after 1865. Indeed, an article written by Lisa Kaiser in the February 3, 2010, edition of *Express Milwaukee* states that Gillespie himself was a leader in the famous Glover case (Kaiser, 2010). Further, it is not beyond reason to think that Booth knew Gillespie from earlier years and recruited him to arrange the Milwaukee Seven meeting in a timed, orchestrated attempt to move the issue forward. Again, no evidence proves this but logic may call for the connection.

It was Booth who went along with Gillespie when he went to register to vote a week before the election on November 7, 1865 (Holzhueter, 1977, p. 181). It can be assumed that this was a preconceived plan put forth by Sherman Booth in collaboration with the *Evening Wisconsin*. It was a plan to set up the court case. Booth had already paid Paine $100 to represent Gillespie after he had convinced the civil rights lawyer that it was possible to change the Supreme Court's decision on the earlier ruling. In addition to witnessing the refusal of Gillespie's registration attempt, Booth then went with Gillespie to the actual polling place on the day of the election. At the polls, Booth witnessed the rejection of Gillespie's right to vote. With Booth's eyewitness account and accompanying documents proving Gillespie was refused the right to vote, Paine filed suit against the members of the Milwaukee Board of Election Inspectors (Holzhueter, 1977, p. 181).

Holzhueter (1977) reports in his article entitled *Ezekiel Gillespie: Lost and Found* that the case, *Gillespie v. Palmer*, moved through the courts unusually rapidly (p. 182). Holzhueter states that this "strongly suggests prearrangement or unusual influence with the Milwaukee County and State Supreme Courts" (Holzhueter, 1977, p. 182). There is no documented evidence of the influence of anyone that would speed the case along; however, due to the recognition of the usual length of time it normally takes to move a case through the system, it would seem that Holzhueter's conclusion would be appropriate. Indeed, Byron Paine had himself been a member of the Supreme Court from 1859 to 1864 and thus would surely have ties to the court and possible influence with its members (Ranney, 1997). It is also interesting to note that Paine rejoined the court in 1867 (Ranney, 1997). Clearly, this opens the door to speculation on favored status or special influence. In any event, on March 28, 1866, the Wisconsin State Supreme Court decided unanimously in favor of Black suffrage. This unanimous decision reversed the Milwaukee County Circuit Court's earlier decision. Wisconsin became just the sixth state in the nation at the time to grant Black Americans the right to vote. Justice Jason Downer delivered the majority opinion:

> To declare a measure or law adopted or defeated—not by the number of votes cast directly for or against it, but by the number cast for and against some other measure, or for the candidates for some office or offices not connected with the measure itself, would not only be out of the ordinary course of legislation, but, so far as we know, a thing unknown in the history of our constitutional law. It would be saying that the vote of every person who voted for any candidate for any office at such an election, and did not vote on the suffrage question, should be a vote against the extension of suffrage. (Ranney, 1997, p. 12–13)

And thus African American male suffrage was established in Wisconsin.

Ezekiel Gillespie's obituary claimed nothing of his part in the case of *Gillespie v. Palmer* nor any of his part in the Underground Railroad or any other civil rights endeavor (Holzhueter, 1977, p. 184). It is one of the reasons the nation is not aware of his contributions to equal/civil rights in America and thus a symbol of his untold story. Holzhueter, a respected scholar and relied on heavily in this chapter, seems to conclude that because Gillespie himself kept quiet about his activities, his family, friends, and all others knew little of his contributions. Generations of Gillespies were unaware of Gillespie's activities regarding this case. According to Holzhueter this meant that Gillespie "well understood his role in the *Gillespie v. Palmer* case" (p. 184). Further he states that Gillespie was "merely the instrument through which Sherman Booth and Byron Paine had secured the franchise for Black men of Wisconsin" (p. 184). One may wonder about these conclusions. Holzhueter's points are arguable. To say that Gillespie was merely a pawn in this action may be short of the truth. Indeed, some authors have claimed that Gillespie's involvement with the abolitionist movement in Milwaukee proved his desire to pursue the case. Didn't he form the committee of seven men in Milwaukee? Though seemingly isolated, this was a blatant act of equal rights advocacy. On the other hand, if he was indeed involved with the Underground Railroad for as far back as at least 1849, this would lead to a more clandestine existence to avoid attracting attention to his part. Thus, he would not remain quiet because he "well understood his role." He would remain quiet to continue his work. Simply playing his role or being "merely an instrument" seems to downplay, indeed devalue, Gillespie's importance in gaining Black suffrage. This doesn't seem like a fair assessment, especially in light of Gillespie being the name of the case that turned the tide and the fact that in the end it was Gillespie who went to the registration station and who went to vote knowing he would be turned down. It may be doubtful that Gillespie, any of his contemporaries, or even Booth and Paine considered him a pawn in someone else's game. Perhaps he, like many African Americans, felt that if too much were made of what he was doing it would not only compromise what he was doing but restrict what he could further do. That is to say that too much exposure would lead to too little accomplishment. Gillespie was not finished with his life's work, clandestine or otherwise, by 1865–1866. Broadcasting himself as a civil rights leader/activist may have altered or put an end to both his civil rights work and possibly his career with the railway. Or maybe Gillespie just didn't like the attention. It is nowhere claimed that he was not a humble man. Many civil rights activists throughout history worked in the shadows and went about their business in covert ways not only for safety and protection but because it was in their nature. Because the personal histories of Booth and Paine are widely known, their motives can't be argued. However, the lack of evidence regarding Gillespie's activities shouldn't exclude recognition of the largely untold part he played in the African American right to vote. Gillespie deserves his recognition as a civil rights advocate and champion of his people. Though *Gillespie v. Palmer* was a decision that only included Wisconsin and only included men, it cannot but have helped the advancement of Black suffrage in other states and for Black women who won their right to vote in 1920.

Glossary

Chicago, Milwaukee, St. Paul Railroad Company: An interstate railroad company operating in the nineteenth century which resulted in the *Milwaukee Road Railroad Company* operated by Alexander Mitchell and partner.

Constitutional Convention: Refers to the 1847–1848 Wisconsin Convention to establish a state constitution to guide the territory into statehood.

Evening Wisconsin: A popular Milwaukee, Wisconsin, newspaper operating from 1847 to 1918 under several titles including *Dailey Life*, *Evening Courier*, *Milwaukee Free Democrats* and well known for social justice beliefs.

Express Milwaukee: Established in 1994, the goal of this newspaper is to provide local news to several communities of the Milwaukee, Wisconsin, metropolitan area.

General Election: An election of the general public for political candidates or selected issues.

Gillespie v. Palmer: This 1866 Wisconsin Supreme Court decision extended Black men the right to vote.

Pawn: Someone or something that can be used to further the cause of another.

Referendum: A general vote by the electorate on a single political question that has been referred to them for a direct decision.

Statehood Convention: Refers to the 1846 Wisconsin Statehood Convention for the purposing of finalizing details of the process of becoming a state and joining the union.

Discussion/Reflection

1. What were the issues and circumstances surrounding your state's preparation to join the union? Did your state have a statehood convention? How was the constitution of your state created? What year was your state admitted to the union?
2. Was your state admitted to the union as a slave state or a free state? What implications were inferred by this status of admission?
3. At what point in your state's history were African Americans and other ethnic minorities allowed to vote? Were suffrage laws in your state gender-specific in the beginning? If so, when did both genders gain the right to vote?
4. How are general elections and referendums run in your state? What are the laws for presenting them for vote and what percentage of the vote is needed to pass the legislation into law?
5. Gillespie had nine children and two stepchildren. What became of them? Perform an online search or contact the State Historical Society of Wisconsin to investigate the lives of the Gillespie children.
6. Does the Chicago, Milwaukee, St. Paul Railroad Company still exist? Are its headquarters still in Chicago? If it still exists, who is its president?
7. In this chapter, we read about Byron Paine and Sherman Booth. We have read about these two in a previous chapter. Create brief biographical sketches for each of these people.

8. Find the legislative record for *Gillespie v. Palmer* and report what new information relating to this chapter that you have found as a result of your investigation.
9. As found in this chapter, in 1889 Ezekiel Gillespie and his wife Catherine established the first American Methodist church in Wisconsin. Investigate to see if it still exists.
10. What is your analysis of the discussion near the end of the chapter which focuses on the question of why Gillespie has been generally unrecognized regarding his role in African American suffrage? Was Gillespie simply a pawn in a larger scheme of things or were there other reasons for his lack of visibility? Support your response with details.

Selected Topics for Further Study

1. History of African American suffrage
2. Supreme Court decisions in your state regarding voting rights
3. The recession of 1857
4. Methodist Episcopal churches
5. *Gillespie v. Palmer*
6. Nineteenth and twentieth century American railroads
7. Issues involving voter discrimination in your state today
8. Lobby groups regarding voters' rights
9. Civil rights voting leaders in your state's history
10. Voter registration laws in your state today

References

Boers, D. (2008). Releasing Joshua Glover: Wisconsin's response to popular sovereignty, states' rights, and the Fugitive Slave Law of 1850. Unpublished manuscript.

Holzhueter, J. O. (1977). Ezekiel Gillespie: Lost and found. *Wisconsin Magazine of History, 180*. Retrieved from http://content.wisconsinhistory.org/cdm/compoundobject/collection/wmh/id/34173/show/34084/rec/2

Kaiser, L. (2010). Ezekiel Gillespie: Milwaukee's champion of African American voting rights. *Express Milwaukee*. Retrieved from http://shepherdexpress.com/print-article-9736-print.html

Harper, D. (2003). RACE in Wisconsin. *Slavery in the North*. Retrieved from http://www.slavenorth.com/wisconsin.htm

Ranney, J. A. (1997). *Gillespie v. Palmer* and others: 28wis.544 (1866). Wisconsin Court System. Retrieved from https://www.wicourts.gov/courts/supreme/docs/famouscases06.pdf

Ranney, J. A. (1995). Looking further than the skin: A history of Wisconsin civil rights law. *Wisconsin Lawyer*, June, 20–53.

Williams, P. W. (2005). Reflections on Wisconsin's *Brown* experience. *Marquette Law Review* 89(1), 7–8.

· 5 ·

MILWAUKEE MOVERS

James Groppi/Vel Phillips

"It was the police who started the fire!"
—Father James Groppi and the NAACP Milwaukee Youth Council, 1967

African Americans have lived in Wisconsin since at least 1746 (Aukofer, 2007, p. 53), and population numbers have steadily increased, especially in Milwaukee, throughout the eighteenth and nineteenth centuries. One reason for Blacks migrating toward Wisconsin was that the politics of Wisconsin were of the progressive doctrine, and it was known that citizens by and large and in certain pockets of the state were openly and eagerly abolitionist. Blacks sought opportunities for freedom in Wisconsin. However, as the 1800s transition into the twentieth century, it seemed that Wisconsin's progressive tendencies regarding human rights were at a standstill. A hopeful beginning for Wisconsin African Americans had slowed to little or no progress on basic civil rights issues such as employment, education, equal opportunity within the community, and housing. Wisconsin seemed to have fallen into step with the discriminating mindset of the rest of the nation. Nevertheless, like many other cities across the nation Milwaukee responded on the backs of local leaders and organizations to attempt to enhance the quality of life for African Americans and advance causes that would bring about change. The struggle was long and difficult but by 1968 changes that would improve the lives for African Americans in Milwaukee and Wisconsin were achieved through a plethora of events and thousands of dedicated individuals lead by dozens of courageous leaders.

Just before the turn of the nineteenth century, Wisconsin passed a law guaranteeing equal access to public accommodations. In 1889, African Americans held a civil rights convention in Milwaukee. Though comparatively small in number, Wisconsin's, and in particular Milwaukee's, African American population was vocal and active in attempting to obtain basic equal rights. For example, in 1835 a Black man voted in the town of Milwaukee's first election (Aukofer, 2007, p. 53). In the 1850s and 1860s, Milwaukeean Ezekiel Gillespie created discussion groups and citizen action committees to push for Black suffrage. On March 28, 1866, in *Gillespie v. Palmer* the Wisconsin State Supreme Court decided unanimously in favor of Black suffrage. Wisconsin became just the sixth state in the nation at the time to grant Black Americans the right to vote. In the twentieth century, Black activism in Milwaukee and Wisconsin continued and increased with far too many people to name in this space. Two people in particular, both addressed later in this chapter, created possibilities for huge gains for African Americans. They were Father James Groppi and Attorney Vel Phillips.

The population of African Americans in Wisconsin steadily grew over the decades. In 1891, 2444 African Americans lived in Wisconsin out of a total population of 1,680,000. In Milwaukee, there were 449 African Americans out of a total population of 204,468 (.22%). The start of World War I (WWI) and the need for workers in the manufacturing sector drew an increase in the number of African Americans working and living in Milwaukee, largely a manufacturing city. Between 1910 and 1920, the population increased by more than 125% but still made up only one-half of one percent of the total population. The African Americans who came to Milwaukee to participate in the WWI manufacturing trade came to a city that was dominated by Germans and highly segregated. By the time of WWI, segregation techniques such as restrictive covenants in deeds and unwritten and unspoken understandings (later referred to as redlining) were used to control the African Americans and corral them into a small, segregated square block area just north of downtown (Aukofer, 2007, pp. 54–55).

The depression years brought forth a substantial increase in the Black population in Milwaukee and an escalation of the segregated housing conditions. In 1930, there were 7501 African Americans living in Milwaukee. Aukofer

(2007) reports that the housing area for these people had also expanded but not by much. It was now four blocks long and three blocks wide. When compared, the population density of this area was twice as much as the average of the rest of the city. It happened that Mayor Daniel W. Hoan ordered a committee to investigate housing in Milwaukee. The committee's report stated that building spacing, heating, and sanitary facilities for many houses were below average. The mayor's response was to order the demolishment of all homes unfit for human habitation. More than half of these houses were occupied by African Americans (Aukofer, 2007, p. 55).

World War II (WWII) caused the same impact on the Black population in Milwaukee as did WWI. War manufacturing brought Blacks up from the Southern states to seek employment in the Northern states' manufacturing industry. These newly arriving Blacks were influenced to live in the same city sector that had always been set aside for African Americans. This sector by the 1950s was being called the inner core. In that year, 21,772 Blacks were living in Milwaukee. This was more than 3% of the total population (Aukofer, 2007, p. 56). The inner core was at this time still not more than one square mile in total size. White Milwaukeeans for the most part ignored Black Milwaukeeans.

Between 1950 and 1960, the Black population increased to 62,458 (Jones, 2005, p. 261). This was now 8.4% of the total population. During this time, the housing status quo remained intact. Because Blacks were denied housing in other parts of the city and in the suburbs due to racism, economics, and discriminatory real estate and loan policies (Jones, 2005, p. 262), they had no choice but to move to the inner core. As more Blacks moved to the inner core, more Whites left the fringes of the inner core. Though since at least as early as 1910, White immigrants, especially Russian Jews (Geenan, 2006, p. 13), also inhabited the inner core and lived and worked alongside of them, Blacks remained the most segregated population among Milwaukeeans. As Whites moved away from the fringes of the inner core, the inner core expanded its boundaries. By 1960, the inner core was calculated to be 5.3 square miles. As 1967 became a landmark year in Milwaukee's Black history, there were 90,000 African Americans living in Milwaukee out of a total population of 777,000 (12%). This 12% of the total population lived in only 5.5% of the total land area of the city. The inner core was estimated to be about 7.9 square miles in 1967 (Aukofer, 2007, p. 57). The result of this was that Milwaukee was one of the most segregated cities in America. The inner core, located on the city's North Side, was home for 90% of Black Milwaukeeans. Employment discrimination, substandard public education, police brutality, and crumbling buildings were prevalent (Jones, 2005, p. 262).

It is in the 1960s that Black activism came to a head in Milwaukee. This is not unlike other Northern cities around the nation. Cities such as Boston, Brooklyn, Newark, Cambridge (MD), Cincinnati, Detroit, and Des Moines responded to the national rise emanating from the South in confronting civil rights issues. Beginning with the establishment of a Milwaukee chapter of CORE (Congress of Racial Equality) in 1963, Black activism steadily rose to its peak in 1967. Housing, also referred to as open housing or fair housing, was one of the issues that garnered major attention. Also in 1963, Black Milwaukee community leaders created a group called The Committee on a Statement of Concern (Aukofer, 2007, p. 66). Playing off a speech by President Kennedy, this group published its own statement on housing which included a plea for fair housing policy via city ordinances in Milwaukee (Aukofer, 2007, p. 67). Over the next five years, multiple committee and activist groups were formed to make the city common council and the mayor respond to the fair housing calls by Black Milwaukeeans. In short, in spite of the valiant efforts by many, the White leaders of Milwaukee stiff-armed and stalled all movement toward open housing or fair housing policies. The mayor, Henry W. Maier, served Milwaukee in that position from 1960 to 1988. Maier was not a popular mayor in the eyes of Black Milwaukeeans. His relationships with the Black community were tense and strained. Most felt that Mayor Maier ignored Black Milwaukeeans and the severe conditions under which they lived. He was not an advocate of civil rights (Metcalfe, 2010d). In fact, it could be said that he was an opponent of any advancement for African Americans. His actions bear that out, at least in the 1960s.

The lessening in the Whites' ability to stiff-arm open housing movements also began in 1963 but did not blossom until 1965 on the way to exploding in 1967. A local Catholic priest, Father James Groppi, was assigned to St. Boniface Church in 1963. St. Boniface was a central city parish on the North Side of Milwaukee. The congregation consisted of African Americans. On summer breaks in 1963, 1964, and 1965, Father Groppi along with other priests went on humanitarian missions to the South where they experienced an escalated amount of discrimination and racism. To the other priests, Groppi stood out as the most focused, intense, and committed believer in working for human rights. Indeed his legacy proves his dedication. As the media was now covering activism and playing a key role in telling and showing the nation what was happening in the South, Father Groppi's involvement brought national attention to the city of Milwaukee. Having experienced the South and having participated in many Southern activities including at Selma and Montgomery and the Beulah Baptist Church Rally lead by Dr. King, he returned to Milwaukee with the intention of following up on his passion for human rights (Jones, 2005, pp. 262–265). At the time a popular slogan was *Why Selma? Why Montgomery?* People were wondering why those cities were centers of activism and other cities were not. Eventually others followed the thinking of Father Groppi when he asked himself *Why Not Milwaukee?* He began by joining the Milwaukee United School Integration Committee (MUSIC). His actions at school building boycotts, construction sights, and at busing demonstrations shocked the locals and made him into a well-known figure throughout the city.

The activism which brought Groppi's most controversy and most success began in 1965 when he joined the NAACP. Because of his work in the South and his remarkable work in Milwaukee with MUSIC, a group of young African Americans asked Father Groppi to be their advisor. These young African Americans were members of the Milwaukee NAACP Youth Council (MYC). They knew Groppi from his work with MUSIC and because at that time he was also NAACP's state youth chairman. By the summer of 1966 Father Groppi, like he did on his missions to the South, put Milwaukee in the national spotlight once again. As events would unfold over the years, he would be seen as most responsible for Milwaukee being dubbed *Selma of the North* (Jones, 2005, p. 278).

Of all the civil rights activism performed by various groups and many key individuals throughout the 1960s in Milwaukee, perhaps two stand out the most and both are related to housing. In 1966, the Milwaukee NAACP Youth Council, advised by Father Groppi, began to protest against exclusionary private membership clubs. One club in particular that drew attention from the MYC was the Fraternal Order of Eagles. The Fraternal Order of Eagles was a national organization and it so happened that Milwaukee had the second largest Eagles Club in the nation. It had 5400 members (Aukofer, 2007, pp. 135–136). The number of members, by itself, did play into the issue but at the root of the issue were two other concerns. First, the Eagles Club represented yet another closed door for African Americans in Milwaukee. Having been excluded from fair housing and having not been able to win fair housing ordinances at the common council or mayor's office, the sting of all exclusionary avenues was intensified. The second issue, the one that became the more important of the two, was the recognition that in Milwaukee the Eagles Club operated as "the old boys' club," especially for politicians and others who could determine circumstances for living in Milwaukee. Politicians couldn't win an election if they didn't join the Eagles Club. The network of members and those who they could influence was too large to win enough votes if you weren't a favored candidate. Non-Eagles were not favored candidates. The result of this power and control of Eagles Club members was that politicians, judges, city controllers, etc., who created policy and law and who judged laws and individuals in court, were affiliated with and ideologically managed by a club that would only allow White people into its membership and refused all other ethnic groups from joining. In short, consideration of all people in all aspects of life was not only ignored but was deemed unnatural and unimportant. Only the White population received consideration in any affair of living. The implications were that discrimination and racism would never be reduced or indeed eliminated under these conditions. For eighteen months over 1966–1967, protests, demonstrations, marches, arrests, firebombings, hearings, meetings, and negotiations occurred in sometimes heated and aggressive fashion. On August 9, 1966, the NAACP Milwaukee Headquarters was bombed. Events became so volatile that Groppi and the MYC felt they needed to establish a Commando unit to deal with difficult situations in protecting activists. This Commando unit, dressed smartly in military-like uniforms, attempted to keep order in picket lines and protect demonstrators from both citizens and police (Metcalfe, 2010b). Several tense confrontations occurred during the time of the Eagles Club demonstrations.

As Metcalfe (2010c) reports, the Milwaukee NAACP Youth Council began by putting pressure on politicians and judges by marching to their houses, protesting their memberships in the Eagles Club, and asking them to justify their memberships in an exclusive club. None of them did. At the city level, the mayor and the common council ignored the protests for as long as they could and then stalled by proposing committees and hearings that were scheduled for a much later date and often not held at all. After significant time and energy was spent by the MYC regarding the Eagles Club, some victories were accomplished by the activists but they were few and small. For example, some local organizations began to cancel meetings at the Eagles Club. It was a long and tenuous protest against the Eagles Club and its symbol of oppression over 1966–1967. The struggle didn't gain the desired outcomes. However, over time the Eagles Club was forced to file bankruptcy based on uncovered debts of $600,000 resulting from the debts and loss of income from event cancellations. This bankruptcy paved the way for the Eagles Club of Milwaukee closing forever in 1988 (Metcalfe, 2010c).

Perhaps the most important civil rights initiative Black activists took on in Milwaukee in the 1960s was again lead by the Milwaukee NAACP Youth Council beginning in the summer of 1967. Still lead by Father Groppi, the MYC decided to focus directly on housing discrimination as their one key issue. To make all Milwaukeeans aware of the issue that Black Milwaukeeans knew too well, MYC members set out to picket the homes of those absentee owners of property in the inner core. As in 1930, the inner core still consisted of a number of houses not suitable for human habitation. The MYC wanted to identify the owners of these houses, mostly White people, and out them to the public while holding them accountable for the awful living conditions within the buildings they owned and rented. For months, MYC members picketed homes and across the city notice was taken. As in almost all of the activities of the MYC, especially after Groppi had established himself as a major motivator for change, media outlets covered the demonstrations that targeted inner core property owners. Also at this time, the NAACP had established a research committee to investigate housing laws in Milwaukee. The committee announced that Milwaukee needed an open housing law. When media covered the committee's recommendation of a campaign for an open housing law in the city of Milwaukee, the whole city started to pay very close attention (Aukofer, 2007, p. 144). In fact, however, an open housing law already existed. In 1965, the state of Wisconsin had passed a law for open housing. However, the law applied to only about 25% of the housing in the state. The percentage was a bit better than 25 in Milwaukee but not enough in the eyes of the Black community. Further, the law only applied to the sale and rental of housing when it was a business. Therefore, the homes of ordinary people did not come under this housing law. Not covered under the law were single-family homes and duplexes of four or fewer units in which the owner lived, owner-occupied homes with four or fewer rooms, and extra homes and cottages on small Milwaukee lots (Aukofer, 2007, p. 144).

It is important to note that prior to 1965, a young, dedicated African American woman had won her way onto the Milwaukee Common Council (MCC). Vel Phillips had encouraged her husband to run for a seat on the Milwaukee Common Council and when he showed no interest, she showed her spunk and wore out three pairs of shoes campaigning for and winning the position (Geenan, 2006, p. 17). She was both the first African American and the first woman to be elected to the MCC. She and her husband had both attended the University of Wisconsin and had both become attorneys. Mrs. Phillips was the first African American woman to earn a law degree from Madison (Dougherty, 2004, p. 35). Mr. Phillips served as Milwaukee NAACP president in the 1950s (Dougherty, 2004, p. 38). Mrs. Phillips would serve sixteen years on the Milwaukee Common Council and then go on to become the first African American judge in Wisconsin as well as the first African American secretary of state (Marsh, 1998, pp. 3–8) . A well-educated, active attorney, Vel Phillips understood housing discrimination and, among many causes she worked to support, housing became one of her most passionate and dedicated interests. In 1962, Vel Phillips became the first alderperson to author and introduce to the Milwaukee Common Council a bill for open housing. Unsurprisingly, the bill, entitled the Phillips Housing Ordinance, was voted down 18–1. Wisconsin state law mandated that a bill could not come up for reintroduction until 90 days had passed since the previous vote. As a result, Alderperson Phillips reintroduced her bill every 90 days for the next five years. The vote continued to be 18–1 (Marsh, 1998, pp. 3–9). The ordinance proposed that the Milwaukee Community Relations Commission, a body of citizen members, be given unprecedented and broad investigative powers in alleged housing discrimination cases. If a particular case was unable to be settled, the city attorney would be asked to initiate court action. Phillips' ordinance also proposed a $250 fine or a thirty-day jail term for convictions. The ordinance applied to anyone renting, leasing, or selling a unit of housing, property, or lot available for constructing a house (Metcalfe, 2010f).

In her years of service before 1967, Vel Phillips was known as a soft-spoken legislator with a cutting-edge mentality that challenged those who opposed her, including mayors. Though her intelligence and education were respected, she was not known as being highly excitable or attention getting. She was a leader not in the Groppi style of aggressive confrontation but rather in a through-the-channels style of negotiation. This changed in 1967 when the Milwaukee NAACP Youth Council declared housing as the primary civil rights issue and pressed for a housing ordinance. In addition to her usual style of working through the channels of change at city hall, Phillips attended MYC strategy meetings to learn how the group would attempt to get a housing ordinance. She marched with the MYC, and she attended protests and demonstrations. She was even among the many who were arrested for her part in activism in favor of fair housing. In gratitude for her dedication to the causes of fair housing and civil rights, Phillips was made an honorary member of the Commandos (Aukofer, 2007, p. 145). She was the only woman ever given this honor.

By 1967, the Milwaukee Common Council had voted 18–1 against the Phillips Housing Ordinance four times. By association, this meant that 18 of 19 aldermen were publicly recognized as opposed to open housing. Of these 18, about six were elected in districts that had Black constituents. Just as in the Eagles Club demonstrations, the MYC began picketing the homes of MCC members. This time, however, after they had marched to the homes and established their presence MYC representatives would actually knock on the doors of the homes to ask why the MCC members had voted against open housing ordinances. The first home picketed on June 19, 1967, belonged to the president of the Common Council, Martin Schreiber. And as in the summer of 1966 with the Eagles Club demonstrations, the picketing of MCC members' homes in 1967 drew wide media coverage which created widespread recognition of the goals of the group.

Schreiber's answer to the MYC was that Milwaukee didn't need to pass an open housing law because the state had already established one in 1965. If the state already had a law, he reasoned, Milwaukee didn't need one. For the rest of June and into July the MYC picketed the homes of five aldermen who had Blacks among their constituents. These aldermen followed Schreiber's lead in answering the Youth Council's questions regarding voting against the Phillips Housing Ordinance. The stiff-arming and stalling by the Milwaukee Common Council was aided by the city attorney who gave the MCC an out by announcing his decision (in response to the MCC asking) that Milwaukee couldn't pass a law that was already passed by the state. This decision was made by the city attorney in spite of the fact that the state attorney general had declared that not only could cities pass a law that was already passed by the state but that the law could be more stringent than the one passed by the state. The alderman and all the other city leaders, including the mayor, simply recited the city attorney's decision whenever they were confronted in giving justification for not voting in favor of the Phillips Housing Ordinance.

The demonstrations continued in the summer of 1967 and went on in mostly peaceful fashion. There was, however, a nervousness about the city as those opposed to open housing began to shadow the Youth Council. Local organizations such as the John Birch Society, the American Nazi Party, and the Ku Klux Klan were opposition groups that began to follow the MYC members and react against them (Jones, 2005, p. 275). In addition, the Milwaukee Police Chief, Harold A. Breier, was fervently opposed to civil rights issues

(Metcalfe, 2010a). Breier served throughout this turbulent period and held the position of police chief from 1964 to 1984. Over the course of his career, he was unwavering in support of the mayor's position regarding advancing civil rights causes. This meant he supported no advancement. Breier began a constant surveillance of the Milwaukee Youth Council and its advisor, Father Groppi. Policemen assigned to the watches would harass MYC members and jail them for such offenses as littering or jaywalking. During the open housing marches, Breier ordered all police officers assigned to protect the Youth Council to not wear police badges so they could not be identified if they were committing acts of police brutality (Metcalfe, 2010e). A normal routine was for the MYC members to march to a house and picket to establish their presence and purpose. They would then knock on the doors to ask the aldermen why they voted against open housing. The doors were either opened or not but no response other than the city attorney's was ever given. After a time, the Youth Council members, escorted by the Commandos, would walk the neighborhoods to show their cause. They would ask homeowners who happened to be out if they would sell or rent their homes to Negroes. Most often, they were given negative answers that included racist language. It was also routine for the MYC to stop in front of some homes and sing civil rights songs. This seemed to increase tension regarding the MYC's presence in the neighborhood. Police were always present.

 One evening the picketing was over and the Youth Council began walking around the neighborhood. They asked the usual questions, received the usual answers, and sang the usual songs. On this evening at one house an incident did occur. As the protestors were singing *We Shall Overcome* in front of a house, a man sitting on the steps of the house became angry, swore at the protestors, and kicked blindly into the group. His kick went into the chest of a small girl. Commandos were on the man in a matter of seconds (Aukofer, 2007, pp. 148–149). Fighting continued for several moments before the police stepped in to stop it. Separating the Commandos from the man, the police took action to quell the disturbance before it turned into a riot—something everyone either wanted or feared in the summer of 1967. The Commandos regrouped and gathered nearby. They were outraged at the incident and were contemplating fighting their way back through the police to bring the man to justice. Before the Commandos had made their decision, Father Groppi, who had already been informed of the incident, came by and met with the Commandos. He helped them to decide not to go back through the police to get this man.

Soon after this event, the Detroit Riot took place. People in Milwaukee watched the violence unfold in Detroit and worried that it would occur in Milwaukee. The summers of 1965, 1966, and 1967 had been a time of escalating civil action and along with the activism came a steady increase in a volatile atmosphere, especially with the number of counterdemonstration groups forming and monitoring the activists. So far in Milwaukee the environment of protest had not broken loose but it seemed likely at any moment. Detroit put a scare not only into the nation as a whole but in particular Milwaukee. Interestingly, during this time the Milwaukee NAACP Youth Council chose not to have any demonstrations or pickets. It was a time of tenseness and anxiety in Milwaukee as most people thought Milwaukee would be the next Detroit; however, things remained relatively quiet. Though seemingly calm at this time, citizens didn't realize that the MYC was planning its next strategy in its struggle to gain an open housing ordinance. The calm in Milwaukee would change.

The strategy that the MYC wanted to implement needed to be, in their eyes, an escalation of the strategy of picketing the homes of aldermen. Aukofer describes the unfolding of the strategy in detail (Aukofer, 2007, Chapter 8). An overview from Aukofer's account is offered here to explain the events through April of 1968.

After lengthy discussions within the group and with their advisor Father Groppi, the Council decided on the strategy of staging an attention-getting march followed by a rally for open housing. The pivotal foundation of this strategy was that the MYC and its supporters would march to a park on the South Side of the city. It was at this South Side park that the MYC would stage its rally. Of great importance in this strategy was that the demonstrators would cross the Menomonee River Valley. The Menomonee River Valley separates the North and South Sides of the city. The inner core was located to the north of the river valley. Lower and middle income Whites lived in the area just south side of the river valley. The South Side consisted of about 350,000 people, about half of which were Polish Americans. Most of Milwaukee still remained populated with people of German descent so both German and Polish Americans populated the South Side. Able to find well-paying factory jobs, these people worked hard, earned a sustainable income, and lived conservatively. They highly resisted the civil rights movement as they feared, among other things, that it would alter their own lives negatively. They especially despised Father Groppi, who by this time by this segment of the population was being called White Nigger (Aukofer, 2007, p. 114).

The South Side was conservative enough to welcome in George Wallace for a presidential campaign rally in 1964. The march and rally planned by the Youth Council for August of 1967 was intended to make a big statement.

August 28, 1967, was a Monday. The Milwaukee Youth Council applied for and was turned down for a park permit to hold a rally at Kosciuszko Park, in the heart of Milwaukee's near South Side. The MYC then applied for a picnic permit at the same park and it was granted. The picnic permit allowed no speeches, singing, or demonstrations. That same evening supporters of open housing joined the MYC on the North Side at Milwaukee's 16th Street Viaduct (Bridge) at about 6:30. The demonstration included approximately 200 marchers. They then began their march to Kosciuszko Park escorted by eight policemen. It was about three miles to the park from the bridge. The route was well known as the local newspapers had published it the day before. Probably because of this, there was an especially large turnout of onlookers and counter-demonstration groups. To the surprise of nearly everyone, an estimated citizen crowd of 5000 people lined the route to Kosciuszko Park. Despite marching the gauntlet between and among 5000 people shouting obscenities, screaming of racism, and holding racist placards, only one small scuffle occurred between the Commandos and the South Side citizens on the way to the park. Police intervened immediately and stopped it. Behind the marchers followed dozens of kids on bicycles.

Reaching the park safely, the Youth Council had realized they had drawn the attention they were seeking. They gathered around Father Groppi and for just a moment began to discuss what to do next. However, there was a problem in doing this. The problem was that a portion of the 5000 people were in the picnic area reserved by city permit for the MYC. The Youth Council felt they weren't being given their rightful space. Father Groppi climbed on to the top of a picnic table and began to speak. Groppi himself and the idea that he was going to address the crowd ignited a roar of anger and threats from the citizen's groups who shouted for him to get down. The demonstrators shouted back. Quickly, before this escalated, the police told Groppi to stop. They told him that he had a picnic permit and that he was not allowed to speak. The police advised him that he was breaking the law. Groppi replied that people were in the picnic space that the group had legally obtained for that day and these people were not welcome there. He told the police to get people out of the picnic area and he would stop speaking. He told the police if they would enforce the law on the people in the picnic area then they could enforce the law on him. In other words, he was saying that if the law wasn't enforced on the citizens it couldn't be enforced on the demonstrators. The law had to be enforced equally. There was a moment of hesitation by all to see what would happen next. Father Groppi made the first move. He had decided that rather than escalating the situation at this point, the demonstrators would take another approach in making their statement. Groppi decided to have the demonstrators leave and he announced this to them, adding to the police that they would be back the next night and they wanted their picnic area to themselves (Aukofer, 2007, pp. 152–153). The demonstrators then headed back toward the 16th Street Viaduct that Groppi had named the Milwaukee Mason-Dixon Line (Metcalfe, 2010g).

The march back to the North Side wasn't so easy. After getting away from the park, about 600 citizens had continued to follow and harass the marchers. The crowd pressed the marchers so closely that now 125 riot police moved them onto the middle of the street to attempt to protect them. Bottles, eggs, rocks, wood, and various other objects were thrown at the marchers. Violence was escalating. The situation was getting out of control. People were going down from the hail of debris while racist slogans were shouted out. Chants erupted as some of the marchers fell under the crush of people and hurled objects. From the citizen groups came such chants as *We want slaves!* and *Get yourself a nigger!* (Aukofer, 2007, p. 153). Other treacherous chants and shouts were heard. Many chants and screams were directed specifically toward Groppi. Along the way a hearse was pushed out into the street to block the marchers. On the hearse was written *Last Ride, Groppi's!* and *White Power!* (Aukofer, 2007, p. 154). As the marchers scrambled to get to the bridge, the police were spraying teargas on the tormenting groups and arresting some of the South Siders. Only when the bridge was reached did the Youth Council members and their supporters feel safe. They knew they could funnel over the bridge and get back to Freedom House. Freedom House was a rented house on the near North Side that served as the headquarters or meeting place of the MYC. As the bewildered Youth Council members and their supporters began to struggle back to Freedom House, they already knew the city had experienced and had responded to their latest attempt to get fair housing in Milwaukee. They wondered what would happen next.

People were expecting trouble the next night as the same 200 marchers began across the 16th Street Viaduct. This time 30 police officers escorted them. In addition, the police had 11 squad cars and three motorcycle police officers in reserve. Reporters from local newspapers were there as were representatives from all other local media outlets. The expected trouble began as soon as the march did. The South Siders were lying in wait and were ready to show the demonstrators what they thought about not just fair housing but the marchers themselves. The details of the horrendous violence and racism that occurred the second night need not be described here except to say that the Monday night atrocities were mild compared to Tuesday night. All forms of Monday violence escalated. Most of the marchers did, under much duress, make it back to the bridge again on Tuesday and scrambled to safety at Freedom House. This was only after many were injured, some were arrested, and all were abused. But when they made it back to Freedom House, the building was set on fire while the Youth Council members were meeting inside it. MYC members were able to get out without injury but the house burned to the ground. Father Groppi and the Youth Council members claimed it was the police who started the fire (Jones, 2005, p. 275). After the house was on fire police refused to allow firefighters in to put it out. Tuesday was a difficult day for the Milwaukee Youth Council.

On Wednesday, August 30, open housing supporters gathered at the burned-out Freedom House. Yet another violent confrontation developed, this time between the police and the people at Freedom House. After Tuesday night's events, the mayor had banned all demonstrations in the city. The Youth Council considered this a blatant attempt to stop open housing demonstrations. With the mayor's ban on demonstrations as the reason, police waded into the group that gathered at Freedom House and began to arrest everyone they could grab. MYC members, including Groppi, feared for their safety and protected themselves by leaving the scene as they could. As the police continued to wade in and arrest people clubs began being used by police to make the arrests. The Youth Council members and supporters who had just been attacked two consecutive nights by citizens were now being attacked by police. During the commotion, Alderperson Phillips arrived for an eyewitness view of what was happening. She pleaded with police to stop. They didn't. She argued for police protection of the MYC members and supporters. They ignored her. Of the 58 people arrested, many had been beaten at the hands of the police. Vel Phillips was outraged at what she had witnessed.

On Thursday, August 31, having nowhere to meet after Freedom House had been burned to the ground, the Youth Council and its supporters turned to St. Boniface Church to hear a speech by Father Groppi. Groppi condemned the racist, violent actions of the citizens during the course of the week's events. He went on to condemn the actions of the police who were clearly not protecting people who deserved protection and who further committed acts of police brutality on the very people they were supposed to protect. He then condemned the mayor for his part in allowing the police and the citizens to do what they did during the marches. Finally, he called out the mayor for his ban on demonstrations as a direct attack on the struggle for fair housing. Alderperson Phillips attended this speech and gave her support to the Youth Council. She was still pushing the Phillips Housing Ordinance and still losing on every vote. After the speech at St. Boniface, the decision was made to march to city hall to protest the mayor's proclamation of no more demonstrations. Four blocks later 137 demonstrators were arrested. Among those arrested were Groppi and Phillips (Aukofer, 2007, p. 164).

For the rest of the summer and fall of 1967 these scenes kept playing out over and over. Groppi and the Youth Council kept the pressure up regarding open housing policy. Vel Phillips kept forcing the vote on the Phillips Housing Ordinance in the Milwaukee Common Council. The mayor and the other aldermen kept stiff-arming and stalling the issue. And the police continued to confront just about anyone who went against the mayor's proclamations. Other notable local Black leaders (Lloyd Barbee, Marilyn Morheuser, Orville Pitts, et. al.) and notable national figures (Dick Gregory, Jesse Jackson, and Martin Luther King) joined the struggle for housing in Milwaukee. A referendum for public housing was called for but denied. Court suits were made on both sides. Most of all, the Youth Council and its supporters kept marching and kept demonstrating. For 200 consecutive nights between August 1967 and March 1968, the Youth Council staged marches and demonstrations. Slowly things began to change. The suburb of Bayside passed the first community open housing law. Feeling the pressure, Milwaukee feigned progress by passing its own open housing law in December of 1967. Progress was dubious because the Milwaukee law was simply a duplicate of the existing state law. Other suburbs slowly began to follow Bayside in passing community laws regarding open housing. By April of 1968, 12 communities had passed open housing laws. Later in the spring of 1968, 17 communities had housing laws on the books. As summer approached, people in Milwaukee reflected on the summers of 1965, 1966, and 1967 and wondered what the summer of 1968 would be like.

April 4, 1968, is a date that no one will ever forget. In spite of what had gone on for the last several years in Milwaukee, no violence occurred on April 4, 1968. There were no lootings, no burnings, no beatings, and no wild demonstrations. Peaceful memorials and vigils occurred throughout the city lead by many Milwaukeeans including Father Groppi and Vel Phillips. In attendance at these ceremonies were Black people, White people, and both Black and White people. On April 8, 15,000 Milwaukeeans quietly walked through the streets of the inner core and downtown Milwaukee (Aukofer, 2007, p. 191). On April 11, President Johnson signed the federal Open Housing Law of 1968 (Aukofer, 2007, p. 192). On April 12, Mayor Maier recommended immediate adoption of the federal law in Milwaukee. On April 30, the Common Council, having elected seven new members on April 2, passed an open housing law that was even stronger than the new federal law (Aukofer, 2007, p. 192). Finally, on July 16, 1968, the Milwaukee County Board of Supervisors passed an all-inclusive housing law covering Milwaukee and its 18 suburbs (Aukofer, 2007, p. 193).

The intense struggle by a dedicated and courageous group of local equal rights activists fighting in their own community for a national agenda regarding a meaningful open housing law had been difficult, but its achievement meant that the obstacle of a legal statute had been conquered. This, of course, paved the way for new local and national struggles in getting the statute enforced.

Glossary

American Nazi Party: An American political party with headquarters in Arlington, Virginia, founded by George Lincoln Rockwell.

Commandos: A unit of people created by the NAACP Milwaukee Chapter Youth Council to protect activists during demonstrations and marches.

Congress for Racial Equality: A U.S. civil rights organization founded in 1942.

Detroit Riot: Also known as the 12th Street Riot, this was a well-publicized incident of looting and violence which lead to civil rights demonstrations in Detroit, Michigan.

Fair Housing Act of 1965: Refers to Wisconsin legislation for open housing that was seen to be discriminating because of its lack of scope and lack of coverage of single family homes, duplexes, and rentals.

Fraternal Order of Eagles: A fraternal club established in 1898 to promote moral character that allowed only White male membership until the 1970s.

Federal Open Housing Law of 1968: Signed into law by President Lyndon Johnson, this legislation was seen to be a comprehensive housing reform act in that it prevented seller/renter discrimination.

Humanitarian Mission: A general term to describe efforts by people to secure health, education, and welfare to those who need it.

Inner Core: A restricted area of the inner city of Milwaukee, Wisconsin, in which African American and other minorities were forced to live because of discriminating housing policies and practices.

John Birch Society: A conservative political organization established in 1958 to combat communism.

Kosciuszko Park: A well-known and popular park in Milwaukee, Wisconsin, named for the Polish military hero General Thaddeus Kosciuszko.

Ku Klux Klan: An extremist right wing secret society in the U. S. organized in the South after the Civil war to establish and hold White supremacy.

Mason-Dixon Line: The boundary between Maryland and Pennsylvania used as the northern limit of the slave holding states before abolition.

National Association for the Advancement of Colored People: Founded in 1909, this organization is the oldest and largest civil rights organization in the U.S.

Phillips Housing Ordinance: First proposed in 1962 and continually proposed until 1967 by Alderperson Vel Phillips, this proposed ordinance (never approved) called for a commission to oversee and decide on housing discrimination issues.

Milwaukee United School Integration Committee: A civil rights activist group in Milwaukee, Wisconsin, which staged demonstrations to end school segregation in the 1960s.

Redlining: To refuse a loan or an insurance policy to people based on race, ethnic background, gender, or other discriminating criteria.

Restrictive Covenants: A covenant imposing a restriction on the use of land so that the value and enjoyment of adjoining land will be preserved.

Segregated Housing: The practice of denying African Americans or other minorities equal access to housing.

Selma of the North: A nickname for the city of Milwaukee, Wisconsin, after civil rights demonstrators were attacked by citizens and authorities in the same way civil rights demonstrators were attacked in Selma, Alabama.

We Shall Overcome: A protest song that has become the key anthem for the African American civil rights movement.

Discussion/Reflection

1. Link the following concepts in a brief narration to form an understanding of the background of the chapter's main purpose:
   a. Northern migration of African Americans
   b. Living locations of immigrant populations
   c. Inner core
   d. Employment and housing discrimination
   e. Substandard education
   f. White flight
2. Investigate the history of housing laws in your state and create a time line of events and legislation.

3. Does it seem logical or absurd to you that virtually all of the authorities in this chapter—mayor, city council, police, fire—were against the movement for fair housing? Explain your perspective.
4. Who were the individuals in your state who were the key leaders in the work for fair housing? Create a brief biographical sketch for just two of them.
5. This chapter mentions Selma and Montgomery, Alabama, as notable cities for humanitarian activism in the 1960s. Describe some events that happened in Selma and Montgomery along these lines and explain why Milwaukee was dubbed *Selma of the North*.
6. The Eagles Club acted as an "old boys' network" to keep oppressed populations oppressed and White elitists in power. Do any of these types of institutions exist today? If so, identify them and discuss with others.
7. Police Chief Harold A. Breier is often called the Bull O' Conner of the North. What do you think this means?
8. The events described in the chapter for the last four days of August, 1967, were surprisingly, not at all unlike the events happening around the country during this time. How do you explain the behavior of the citizen's groups and the counterdemonstrators as we see them during these four days in this chapter?
9. The last line of the chapter opens our eyes to a new line of concern. What are the implications of its meaning?
10. Right now, in your own state, what are the issues being addressed or identified regarding discriminating practices? Explain them if you can.

Selected Topics for Further Study

1. Northern migration of African Americans—1940s, 1950s, and 1960s
2. James Groppi
3. Vel Phillips
4. Discriminatory real estate and loan practices
5. Congress on Racial Equality
6. National Association for the Advancement of Colored People
7. President Kennedy
8. Beulah Baptist Church
9. Civil rights actions in the South—1960s

10. Phillips Housing Ordinance
11. John Birch Society
12. American Nazi Party
13. Ku Klux Klan
14. Civil rights songs—1940s, 1950s, and 1960s
15. Detroit Riot—1967
16. George Wallace
17. Mason-Dixon Line
18. Martin Luther King
19. President Johnson
20. Civil rights activism in the history of your state/town

References

Aukofer, F. A. (2007). *City with a chance: A case history of civil rights revolution*. Milwaukee: Marquette University.

Dougherty, J. (2004). *More than one struggle: The evolution of Black school reform in Milwaukee*. Chapel Hill: University of North Carolina.

Geenan, P. H. (2006). *Images of America: Milwaukee's Bronzeville 1900–1950*. Chicago: Arcadia.

Jones, P. (2005). Not a color but an attitude: Father James Groppi and Black power politics in Milwaukee. In Jeanne Theoharis & Komozi Woodward (Eds.), *Groundwork: Local Black freedom movements in America* (pp. 259–282). New York: New York University.

Marsh, C. (1998). *Vel Phillips: African American politician*. Peach Tree City, Georgia: Gallopade International.

Metcalfe, E. (2010a). Breier, Harold A. *The March on Milwaukee Civil Rights History Project*. Retrieved from http://uwm.edu/marchonmilwaukee/keyterms/breier/

Metcalfe, E. (2010b). Commandos, National Association for the Advancement of Colored People Youth Council. *The March on Milwaukee Civil Rights History Project*. Retrieved from http://uwm.edu/marchonmilwaukee/keyterms/?fwp_paged=2

Metcalfe, E. (2010c). Eagles Club. *The March on Milwaukee Civil Rights History Project*. Retrieved from http://uwm.edu/marchonmilwaukee/keyterms/eagles-club/

Metcalfe, E. (2010d). Maier, Henry W. *The March on Milwaukee Civil Rights History Project*. Retrieved from http://uwm.edu/marchonmilwaukee/keyterms/maier-henry/

Metcalfe, E. (2010e). Milwaukee Police Department. *The March on Milwaukee Civil Rights History Project*. Retrieved from http://uwm.edu/marchonmilwaukee/keyterms/mpd/

Metcalfe, E. (2010f). Open housing ordinance: Introduction in Milwaukee. *The March on Milwaukee Civil Rights History Project*. Retrieved from http://uwm.edu/marchonmilwaukee/keyterms/open-housing-ordinance/

Metcalfe, E. (2010g). South side. *The March on Milwaukee Civil Rights History Project*. Retrieved from http://uwm.edu/marchonmilwaukee/keyterms/south-side/

· 6 ·

ATTORNEY FOR THE PLAINTIFFS

Desegregating Milwaukee Public Schools

"I see myself as a human being, interested in humanity and fulfilling its maximum potentialities. I realize this will never happen as long as whites view themselves as being superior because of their whiteness—therefore I must fight racism."
—Lloyd Barbee, 1969

By all accounts, Lloyd Barbee was a cultured intellectual who possessed grand powers of articulation that brought people to notice. When people remember Lloyd Barbee and talk about the monumental civil rights work that he accomplished, they never fail to mention the persuasive powers of his use of language and vocabulary. He combined intellectual power with articulation power and this, supported by a phenomenal inner drive dedicated to human justice, carried him to being a difference maker in the time that he served. He loved classical music, opera, and the theater and knew them so well that he could be heard singing his favorite operas or reciting Shakespearean sonnets even as he climbed the steps of the courthouse. He was a cultured man—some say even a cultural "elitist" (Miner, 2013a, p. 38)—but he was driven by his sense of human justice. He believed that all humans had inalienable rights because they were humans. He shared the ideas given down by his father, Earnest, who taught him to live by the motto *Be right or get right. And when you are right, go ahead* (Miner, 2013a, p. 37). Earnest Barbee had a strong belief in human rights and social justice and lived according to his beliefs. He opposed the constant domination of White ideological management and this opposition was evident in the Barbee home. Later in his life, Lloyd would look back upon his father's influence and say "I see myself as a human being, interested in humanity and fulfilling its maximum potentialities. I realize this will never happen as long as whites view themselves as being superior because of their whiteness—therefore I must fight racism" (Miner, 2013b, p. 2). Young Lloyd couldn't help but follow his father's lead and carried the torch for both of them all of his life. His passion for justice was obvious. Barbee was so adamant in his beliefs and so skilled at making his points that he was often seen as overzealous and confrontational, especially when he made blistering attacks on his opponents such as fellow politicians, mayors, school board members, superintendents, or anyone in opposition to his thinking. He challenged people with a cutting-edge intellect that, though reasoned and logical, seared to the very bones of the people he challenged (Dougherty, 2004, p. 72).

Born in Memphis, Tennessee, in 1925, Barbee grew up under Jim Crow segregation, which found him walking past several White schools while on his way to his own all-Black school. This was not a unique experience for Black students at the time; however, Barbee, acutely aware of the injustice of it because of his father's upbringing (his mother had died when he was six months old), had a difficult time accepting the situation (Miner, 2013a, p. 37). When he faced the additional insult of not being able to use the local public library, it was time for young Lloyd to do something about it. At 12-years-old while still in middle school, Lloyd Barbee joined the National Association for the Advancement of Colored People (NAACP). Little did he know at the time that he would be a lifetime member of the NAACP and rise to many important positions, including Wisconsin state president. At age 17, while still in high school, another revealing experience occurred for Barbee. A well-known Black activist speaker (A. Philip Randolph) was in Memphis and wanting to present some lectures at local Black churches to spur people to pursue their civil rights. The church leaders refused to allow the lectures. Barbee's sensitivities were heightened and, even at age 17, he was outraged at the church leaders for being afraid to allow the activist to speak at service. He couldn't understand why the church leaders allowed the Black community to be defeated. He declared that the church leaders had no backbone (Ranney & Aldridge-White, 2004, p. 2).

From 1943 to 1946, Barbee served in the United States Navy. When he was on leave, he would visit relatives who had settled in the Wisconsin cities of Milwaukee and Beloit. This allowed him to become familiar with the state that he would eventually move to and within which he would spend the rest of his life. But first he completed his Navy career and next he enrolled and graduated from LeMoyne College in Memphis (since 1968, Lemoyne-Owen College). He studied social science and majored in economics. Upon graduation from LeMoyne in 1949, Barbee was recognized for his academic and intellectual prowess and was granted a scholarship to the University of Wisconsin–Madison (UW–Madison). It was during this time at UW–Madison that Barbee realized that Southern racism wasn't particular to the South. In his first year in school, he found that not only fellow students were racist, but also the professors treated him in racist ways as well. For these reasons, Barbee dropped out of UW–Madison after his first year. He joined the Americans for Democratic Action and became a student activist in Madison. After a short while he realized that a law degree would be useful and increase his power and ability to work for human rights and so soon he returned to UW–Madison. He finished his law certificate in 1955 and his LL.B. in 1956 (Lloyd A. Barbee Papers, n.d.).

By 1957, Barbee had established employment as a law examiner for the Industrial Commission of the Wisconsin Unemployment Compensation Department. He also served as chairman of the Mayor's Commission on Human Rights and as legal consul to the Governor's Commission on Human Rights (Lloyd A. Barbee Papers, n.d.). These positions gave Barbee ample opportunity to experience direct observation of the injustices of employment and housing—two issues Barbee would be involved with for the rest of his life. In fact, probably his first claim to fame came in 1961 when he organized a 13-day around-the-clock sit-in at the Wisconsin state capitol in Madison to convince the legislation to pass a fair housing act (Dougherty, 2004, p. 75). It seems notable that he was employed by the state when he conducted this sit-in as it provides another early example of Barbee standing by his beliefs no matter possible ramifications of doing so. Though the sit-in was unsuccessful at getting a law passed at that time, it gained attention for the cause and Barbee would later play a large role in getting the 1965 Fair Housing Act approved through the state legislation.

While he was attending the UW–Madison Law School, Barbee continued to be active in the NAACP and the issues of concern for the organization. In fact, in 1955 he became president of the Madison Chapter of the NAACP. While in his law studies, he conducted research into housing laws and practices in Madison. As part of his studies, he even produced a documentary film on housing discrimination in Madison, which in later years the university refused to allow him to use (Lloyd A. Barbee Papers, n.d.). People were noticing the work he was doing to advance the causes of human rights and social justice. One of those people was Milwaukee Assemblyman Isaac Coggs, who was working for stronger enforcement of Wisconsin fair employment laws. Coggs and some others sought out Barbee and established a relationship that lead to Coggs influencing Barbee to move to Milwaukee and run for the assembly (Ranney & Aldridge-White, 2004). It didn't take long for Barbee to agree. After being chosen as NAACP state president in 1961, Barbee took the encouragement from Coggs and moved to Milwaukee in late fall 1962. Here he started his life's work in Milwaukee that lead him to be a difference maker for decades regarding causes related to human, civil, and social rights. When he got to Milwaukee, he quickly realized he had moved into a hotbed of justice/equity issues that included not only fair housing and employment, but a strikingly discriminating educational arena. It didn't take long for Lloyd Barbee to have an impact in Milwaukee. He was almost immediately chosen to run the Milwaukee branch of the NAACP, and in 1964, he was elected to the 18th Assembly wherein he served for six consecutive terms (Miner, 2013a, p. 38). The 18th Assembly District was near downtown Milwaukee and the seat of the inner core which had suffered longtime housing and employment discrimination as well as the related issues falling out from that discrimination impacting local schools and the education, especially, of Black children. Barbee earned the respect of his constituents through his activism and thus had wide leeway in what he could propose and how he could go about winning his proposals. In short, after the first few months of his first term, and especially after his work in 1963, Barbee had earned himself a free hand. This is not to say he didn't ruffle feathers via issues and his confrontational techniques, and this is not to say he didn't have people, both Black and White, on all sides of issues disagreeing with him, but it is to say the combination of active participation in crucial issues and the demanding, diligent, persistent insistence on accomplishing his goals through reason, logic, and, if necessary, civil disobedience, earned Barbee the respect of the majority of Milwaukee's Black population and especially the 18th Assembly. For the first time, it seemed to them, they had a representative who would speak truth to power and act on that truth. Though active in a plethora of issues, Barbee may be most remembered for his work toward the desegregation of Milwaukee Public Schools (MPS).

In the years previous to Barbee's arrival in Milwaukee, the Milwaukee Public School System had established a procedure that was meant to comply with the Supreme Court decision of 1954, *Brown v. Board of Education*. The decision overturned the *1896 Plessy v. Ferguson* decision, which had declared that separating facilities for Blacks and Whites was legal. Brown called for an end to segregated public facilities and expected that desegregation be arranged immediately. The procedure MPS used for its response to the *Brown* decision, known as *intact busing*, was a plan that had buses picking up Black students at their home schools and transporting them to White schools. In the White schools, the Black students would take classes only with each other and then at the end of the day would be bused back to their home schools (Milwaukee, 2010). It was even fairly common that the Black students would be bused back to their home schools for lunch and then returned again for afternoon classes at the White schools. The Board of Directors (Board of Education [School Board]) of the Milwaukee Public School System reasoned that this intact busing procedure was school desegregation according to *Brown*. Barbee and local Black leaders didn't agree. In 1963, Barbee demanded that a better busing plan be implemented for the purpose of desegregation. He went to the Milwaukee School Board and offered his own plan that he called *selective busing* in which a more genuine student exchange would take place (Ranney & Aldridge-White, 2004, p. 4). The genuine student exchange being referred to was that of full, or at least more, participation in integrated school activities. The Milwaukee School Board, via its Special Committee on Equality of Educational Opportunity (eventually known as the Story Committee), rejected his plan stating that neighborhood schools had to be preserved at all costs (Dougherty, 2004, p. 88). It was clear to Barbee and most others that the school board committee and thus the school board itself was saying that they would keep the status quo (segregated schools) in the name of neighborhood schools. In particular, the Special Committee on Equality of Educational Opportunity led by Harold Story—a man who paralleled Lloyd Barbee in confrontational technique—would continue to stiff-arm and oppose Barbee, the NAACP, and the Black community in every effort toward desegregation of public schools. Many volatile meetings took place at which Barbee and Story battled each other regarding school desegregation. They each knew they were the primary leaders for the respective sides of this monumental school/society issue and they both took it personally. In one particular instance on January 21, 1964, Barbee walked out of a committee meeting after a confrontation with Harold Story regarding the seating arrangements. Story was trying to move

Barbee away from the rest of his constituency so as to isolate him in preparation for an interrogation Story had planned for him (Civil Rights Activists, n.d.). This set the stage for years of struggle regarding Milwaukee school desegregation. Lloyd Barbee led that struggle for those who dreamed of desegregation as a basic human and civil right.

Shortly after MPS rejected his selective busing plan for desegregation and refused to budge on intact busing, Barbee was invited to speak at a Milwaukee Junior Bar Association luncheon (Dougherty, 2004, p. 71). This was a group of White lawyers who were expecting Barbee to bring them up to date on racist atrocities in the South. To their great surprise, Barbee told them about racist atrocities in the North—in their own city of Milwaukee. Barbee used the *Brown* case to mean that segregation was illegal everywhere, not just in the South, and that, thus, the de facto segregation in MPS was in violation of the U.S. Supreme Court decision in *Brown* and against the 14th Amendment of the U.S. Constitution. Intact busing was a violation of federal law and needed to be stopped. Further, he described several examples of discrimination in other areas of the schools such as buildings and grounds and classroom features and teachers. In particular, he made a case against all-Black schools, all-White schools, and Black-only teachers for Black-only schools. The Junior Bar Association was stunned by his speech. Barbee had made his points. In addition, Barbee had won some allies and in the least broadened the conversation about an issue that the Milwaukee Public School System was most happy to keep unknown or at least left alone as it had been for over a decade. However, Barbee's appearance at the Junior Bar Association luncheon didn't only bring broader light on the issue of school segregation within the community of Milwaukee lawyers. More importantly, it seems, the speech resulted in the school board making a tactical error that allowed Barbee and his followers to gain ground. The Special Committee on Equality of Educational Opportunity of the Milwaukee School Board decided to respond to the speech that Barbee gave. The committee claimed that what Barbee was addressing was not a school issue but a housing and neighborhood issue. It claimed that the busing plan Barbee offered would be unfair to all students and that Barbee should be attacking job and housing discrimination, not school segregation (Dougherty, 2004, p. 73). This response by MPS joined Black leaders and Black citizens in a larger, more comprehensive, more unified approach to attempt to gain equality via desegregation. It also increased the number of Whites drawn to the struggle.

In that same notable year of 1963, Barbee had, as state president of the NAACP, communicated with Department of Public Instruction (DPI)

Superintendent Angus B. Rothwell. He requested that the state superintendent deliver an order eliminating de facto segregation in all Wisconsin schools. Rothwell accepted Barbee's proposal for consideration but replied that he needed proof that de facto segregation indeed existed. That proof needed to include intent and illegality. Rothwell agreed to investigate. In September, completing his investigation, Rothwell informed Barbee that he had found no intentional segregation by MPS officials. He therefore would create no DPI proposal for banning de facto segregation in Wisconsin schools. Rothwell, however, included in his report that he wondered if the alteration of school boundary lines by the MPS Board of Education was within Wisconsin state law (Lloyd A. Barbee Papers, n.d.). A significant event of the next turbulent year, 1964, was the election of Barbee as president of an organization called the Milwaukee United School Integration Committee (MUSIC). MUSIC consisted of a coalition of civil rights workers, religious leaders, and labor organization leaders whose combined mission was to perform reasoned and moral persuasion to gain desegregation litigation (Milwaukee, 2010).

Barbee didn't always embrace the less-militant stances thus far taken by other leaders in the Milwaukee struggles for human rights and social justice. He believed that when reason alone failed action must be taken. In this thinking, and when he led MUSIC, Barbee didn't leave out civil disobedience as a technique in promoting human rights. He promoted and used himself such tactics as sit-ins, boycotts, demonstrations, bus blocking, construction stoppage, and other means for the purposes of getting laws changed and equity established. In fact, MUSIC incorporated all of these techniques, which gained much attention around the city and drew national media coverage that not only identified the issues but allowed a platform for offering solutions. In the course of these actions many citizens were arrested, including Barbee. One example occurred on May 24, 1965, as Barbee and eight other MUSIC demonstrators linked arms in front of a school bus to block it against its departure. All nine protestors were arrested on the spot as, one-by-one, police officers carried the protestors to the police vans and took them to jail (Miner, 2013a, pp. 49–50).

One of the first initiatives MUSIC undertook was to send a delegation to local schools to investigate the conditions that existed. In the course of this investigation, evidence of inequities was found regarding many elements of schooling between Black schools and White schools and among MPS schools in general. The patterns were obvious. To illustrate the problems, MUSIC created a massive boycott of MPS schools. To accommodate law and students' learning and to show the importance of education, MUSIC undertook the huge job of creating alternative schools, called Freedom Schools (Miner, 2013a, pp. 29–32). Many and various individuals and groups joined the local clergy in creating Freedom Schools with educational curriculum to include Black Studies. The boycott was an iconic event that shook the Milwaukee citizenry and heightened the attention to equity issues. By this time and into 1965, MUSIC and several other Milwaukee civil rights groups (CORE, Northside Non-Partisan Conference, Milwaukee Youth Council, and NAACP) were putting immense pressure on MPS officials (Aukofer, 2007, Chapter 6). In October of 1965, MUSIC called for another massive school boycott and another round of Freedom Schools. Again, the boycott was seen as a success in shaking the city into action regarding inequality and the social injustice of desegregation. Shortly after this second boycott, Lloyd Barbee, as lead attorney of six others, filed suit on behalf of the parents of thirty-two Black students and nine White students to force the Milwaukee School Board to end its segregation practices. It would be a monumental lawsuit lasting for years, dominating Barbee's life, and ending in controversy.

The lawsuit was named *Amos et al. v. Board of School Directors of the City of Milwaukee*. The Amos children attended MPS and were chosen to be named in the suit. The lawsuit was the first in the nation of its kind to include both Black and White children. The lawsuit alleged that school authorities maintained or fostered segregation by the following ways:

- Establishing school boundary lines based on segregated housing patterns
- Permitting the easy transfer of White students to other schools
- Assigning Black students to racially segregated schools
- Approving plans to build schools that were predominantly Black
- Failing to integrate inner core area students transferred by bus from their own to another school (Lloyd A. Barbee Papers, n.d., The Milwaukee School Desegregation Case section, para. 3)

Within the lawsuit itself, the Black community was particularly concerned about intact busing. The plaintiffs sought:

- Injunctions against school officials
- A school desegregation plan
- Redrawing of school boundary lines
- Construction of new schools to promote integration (Lloyd A. Barbee Papers, n.d., The Milwaukee School Desegregation Case section, para. 4)

Within the lawsuit, evidence was presented to show that 14 of 21 elementary schools within the inner core were cited as having Black enrollments exceeding 90%, six schools having Black enrollments over 50%, and one school having Black enrollments over 40%. Similar patterns were shown for junior and senior high schools in the inner core. Of 120 MPS schools *outside* the inner core, 106 had Black enrollments of less than 10%. In 1968, after Barbee had conducted a major research investigation and gained even more evidence of segregation, an amended complaint was filed. In 1973, eight years after the complaint was filed, the trial began (Lloyd A. Barbee Papers, n.d.).

In January, 1976, after arguments were heard back and forth for three years and after having studied the case presented to him, Federal District Judge John Reynolds ruled in favor of Barbee and the plaintiffs. Judge Reynolds found that MPS was illegally segregated and in violation of the 14th Amendment. He ordered that the Milwaukee School Board take immediate action to desegregate its schools. Cited in the judge's ruling were the following:

- MPS used substandard classrooms, busing patterns, student transfers, and personnel patterns meant to keep students in schools separated by race
- MPS used Black school buildings that were older than White school buildings and that were overcrowded
- MPS built additions to existing schools in Black areas rather than to reassign students or redraw school boundary lines to solve overcrowding
- MPS permitted boundary line changes to allow White students to attend White schools
- Intact busing, by its history, was not temporary
- MPS used an open transfer policy that favored Whites in that Whites could transfer out but Blacks could not transfer in
- MPS spent more money on White schools
- MPS assigned teachers with more experience to White schools (Lloyd A. Barbee Papers, n.d., The Milwaukee School Desegregation Case section, paras. 6 and 7)

Judge Reynolds established a three-year desegregation plan and assigned a Special Master (John Gronouski) to monitor and guide the plan. Based on the magnet school concept, it was to begin in September, 1976. By this time, the name of the case had been changed to *Armstrong v. O'Connell* because all of the Amos children had graduated.

The Milwaukee Public School Board appealed the decision to the U.S. Supreme Court. The appeal was won in 1978 on the grounds of insufficient evidence. The Supreme Court set aside Reynold's decision and remanded the case for retrial back to the district court for reconsideration. The Supreme Court held that more evidence was needed to prove intent, especially in relation to intact busing. The district court had to prove not only the school board's intent to segregate but also the specific results of that intent. In the retrial, Barbee focused on two primary objectives. First, he bolstered his evidence with more documentation of segregated practices and established more personal testimony in support of the plaintiff's case, including the testimony of one key witness who was formerly a member of the Milwaukee School Board and specifically addressed intact busing and its consequences. Barbee was focusing on proving intent to segregate and the present effects of the segregation. Second, he offered more plans for remedy of the situation. In February of 1979, Judge Reynolds ruled that the board had used intent to segregate MPS since 1950 and the present results of that segregation were system wide. Barbee and the plaintiff's had prevailed again (Lloyd A. Barbee Papers, n.d.).

On March 1, 1979, an out of court agreement was reached upon which a settlement was made. The settlement called for a five-year desegregation plan. The end product of the plan was that twenty all-Black schools would be allowed to remain but no all-White schools would be permitted. The settlement did not specify many of the complaints filed in the original suit. In May of 1979, Judge Reynolds accepted the settlement. In June 1979, the NAACP appealed the desegregation plan stating that it discriminated against Black students forced to remain in all-Black schools (Lloyd A. Barbee Papers, n.d.). Barbee had retired from the Assembly in 1977 to devote more time to the lawsuit. He continued to be the attorney for the plaintiffs and worked tirelessly for the cause of eradicating segregation in the Milwaukee Public Schools. When the settlement of 1979 took place, he removed himself from the case. After that, he continued his law practice and taught in the Department of African American Studies at the University of Wisconsin-Milwaukee.

A human rights legend in Milwaukee, Lloyd Barbee died in 2002. Though he would be the first to admit that his school desegregation efforts did not result in the final goal, he would want to acknowledge that work done toward that goal gained ground toward a justified end. In Milwaukee, it is hoped that the work of Lloyd Barbee and so many others would be rekindled to begin to establish the justified end desired for what is considered today to be the most segregated school system in America.

Response to the Settlement of 1979

The five-year desegregation plan called for in the settlement of 1979 remained in effect until July 1, 1984. A key to understanding desegregation efforts during and after this time is to understand the evolution of another aspect of Barbee's work toward ending segregation in Milwaukee. In the 1976–1977 school year, Barbee lobbied legislators to support an integration aid program entitled Chapter 220. The idea behind Chapter 220 was to transfer low-income students within school districts and between school districts for the purpose of promoting cultural and racial integration (Wisconsin Legislative Fiscal Bureau, 2005, p. 1). There was a qualifier on each end of the entitlement for each partner in the program. As this was to be a voluntary program, students could not be forced to participate and only would participate if they so desired. On the other hand, school districts and schools within school districts could not be forced to participate unless they deemed there was an educational purpose to implementing and engaging in a student transfer (Wisconsin Legislative Fiscal Bureau, 2005, p. 1). In this fashion, the legislation Barbee and others were lobbying for was voluntary on both sides of the entitlement. Because this program called for state funding, the idea was that racial balance could be achieved at no cost to local taxpayers and, indeed, supported state aid for school district participation, thus providing a monetary incentive for districts to participate (Wisconsin Legislative Fiscal Bureau, 2005, p. 1).

While the 1979 settlement was in effect (1979–1984), the legislature enacted Chapter 220. This was noticed around the nation because of the uniqueness of a state government encouraging school desegregation, especially via the use of state monies. Though Lloyd Barbee had removed himself from the case after the 1979 settlement, his presence could still be felt as events unfolded after 1979.

In addition to the enactment of Chapter 220 and continued lobbying for desegregation efforts and legislation, another lawsuit was filed in federal district court by the Milwaukee Public School System. This case was brought forth in 1984 as a complaint against 24 suburban Milwaukee school districts and the state of Wisconsin (Kava, 2009, p. 1). Once again, the case was filed to question the status of segregated schools in Milwaukee and to claim that MPS was in defiance of the 14th Amendment, the U.S. Constitution, and the *Brown* decision. The plaintiffs called for increased integration of MPS. This 1984 federal court case became known as the Milwaukee School Desegregation Case (Kava, 2009, p. 1). In 1987, the court approved a settlement that called for Chapter 220 to facilitate and finance increases in the number of voluntary transfers between MPS and suburban school districts. The settlement was implemented until it expired in 1993 and then was extended until 1995. Since 1995, the Milwaukee Public School System has negotiated individual transfer agreements with suburban schools (Kava, 2009, p. 12). This practice has created a situation whereby suburban schools have profited greatly from Chapter 220 funding.

It can be seen from the aforementioned overview of Chapter 220 that because of his continued involvement with that program, Barbee continues to influence desegregation efforts in public schools. A significant turn in this road must also be pointed out to achieve a fuller view of post-Barbee desegregation efforts. Barbee's focus was on desegregating MPS as a public school district. His goal was to desegregate the local public schools to give the fairest chance for all the school district's children to get an equal education and future opportunity. Barbee never backed off of this goal and worked until he died for its achievement. He didn't want to consider other ways to gain equal education until he had exhausted all hope of public school desegregation. Meanwhile, White flight was escalating and segregation was increasing. White flight to suburbs created city schools with more than 50% Black students (Ranney, n.d., p. 1). Citizens and legislators began to see this as indication that the desegregation efforts had failed to this point and that another way of obtaining the goal had to be created. If progress hadn't been made something else had to be tried. A groundswell of support for a choice school system began. The idea was that legislation should be passed so that parents could have a choice of what schools their children could attend. First called the Milwaukee Parental Choice Program, a massive campaign was implemented both city wide and throughout the state. The program was unique within the entire nation because it called for parental choice of either public or private schools. By the end of the 1980s, a highly influential school choice movement had developed, and by 1992, the Wisconsin Supreme Court had upheld a choice program that allowed students to attend both public and private schools via state financial vouchers (Ranney, n.d., p. 1). The inclusion of private schools in a state education spending budget was controversial enough; however, more controversy developed by the end of the 1990s when these private schools could also include parochial schools (Ranney, n.d., p. 1).

In 2017, Milwaukee's progress toward desegregation in its public schools relies mostly on the same Chapter 220 legislation Barbee supported in 1976. If he were alive today, he would say it wasn't enough. Indeed, by 2014, MPS was considered to be one of the most segregated school systems in America (Richards and Mulvaney, 2014, p. 1). Currently, the percentage of Black children attending intensely segregated schools (defined below) is about the same as it was in the 1960s (Richards and Mulvaney, 2014, p. 1). According to a May, 2014, article in the *Milwaukee Journal-Sentinel Newspaper*, the following are derived from enrollment analysis:

- One of three MPS students today attends a school that is intensely segregated, defined as any school with an enrollment that is at least 90% one race.
- In MPS 46% of Black students attend an intensely segregated Black school.
- Nearly one in five Hispanic students attends an intensely segregated Hispanic school. (Richards and Mulvaney, 2014, p. 2)

This same article reports that the very school named after Lloyd Barbee has a Black enrollment of 92% (Richards and Mulvaney, 2014). Lloyd Barbee himself would be intensely disappointed.

Glossary

14th **Amendment:** Adopted in 1868, this amendment guarantees the Bill of Rights, especially regarding due process and equal protection under the law.

18th **Assembly:** The Milwaukee, Wisconsin, legislative district serving the inner core during the 1960s.

Americans for Democratic Action: An American political organization advocating progressive policies including economic and social equality.

Amos et al. v. Board of School Directors City of Milwaukee: This 1965 lawsuit brought forth by Lloyd Barbee and others sought to end segregation in Milwaukee, Wisconsin, schools.

Armstrong v. O'Connell: Refers to the 1976 name change of the *Amos et al. v. Board of School Directors City of Milwaukee* court case.

Brown v. Board of Education: The landmark 1954 U.S. Supreme Court decision regarding African American segregation and declaring that separate was not equal.

De Facto Segregation: In practice, regardless of law, segregation can be proven to occur and cause impact.

Department of Public Instruction: Refers to the Wisconsin state organization for the overview of state education, including laws and funding.

Freedom Schools: Temporary free schools set up by civil rights activists for African Americans as part of a civil rights movement to end school segregation.

Intact Busing: Busing African Americans to White schools to attend segregated classes.

Injunction: A judicial order that restrains an action deemed unlawful by the court.

Junior Bar: An associate attorney who normally does not hold ownership interest in a law firm.

LeMoyne College: A private liberal arts church-affiliated college located in Memphis, Tennessee, serving primarily African American students established in 1871 but merged with Owen College in 1968 to become LeMoyne-Owen College.

***Milwaukee Journal-Sentinel*:** The primary Milwaukee, Wisconsin, newspaper with the largest circulation in the state and which is circulated widely throughout the state.

Milwaukee Parental Choice Program: A school program which allows low-income children to attend public, private, and parochial schools of their choice.

Milwaukee School Desegregation Case: A 1984 complaint against 24 suburban schools calling for increased integration between city and suburban schools and considered to be the vehicle that escalated the operation of Chapter 220.

***Plessy v. Ferguson*:** The landmark 1896 U.S. Supreme Court decision regarding African American segregation and declaring that separate was equal.

Selective Busing: A plan put forth by Lloyd Barbee to bus African American students to White schools where they would be immersed into all aspects of the White school culture and programs.

Discussion/Reflection

1. Barbee believed that all humans had inalienable rights because they were human. Do you agree? If so, what rights do you think are inalienable? If not, why not?
2. What does it mean to "speak truth to power and then act on that truth"? Can you think of times throughout history that a person or people have spoken truth to power and acted on it? Briefly describe.
3. Has there been a time when you have spoken truth to power and then acted on it? Describe.
4. As you read this chapter what did you learn about the American judicial system by following the case of *Amos et al. v. Board of School Directors City of Milwaukee*?
5. Were Freedom Schools examples of self-imposed segregation or were they a vehicle to make a point? Explain your perspective.
6. Were you surprised at the settlement of 1979? Did you expect it? What are your opinions of Chapter 220? For example, should Chapter 220 be state funded, should suburban schools be allowed to profit from it, is it effective at meeting its stated goals?
7. The Milwaukee Parental Choice Program (MPCP) described in this chapter was the first of its kind in the nation and continues to be one

of the largest school choice programs in America. What are your views of the concept in general and of the particular aspects of MPCP?
8. The chapter includes the notion that neighborhood schools are segregated schools. Explain what that means and why that is.
9. Barbee devoted a major portion of his life to end segregation. In the end, he didn't accomplish what he wished to accomplish. What advice based on Barbee's work would you give to others who may be considering involvement in social justice issues?
10. At this time there can be found many articles, essays, columns, websites, and books asserting that American citizens, including ethnic minorities, desire to "resegregate" America. What does this mean and what response do you have to it?

Selected Topics for Further Study

1. A. Philip Randolph
2. LeMoyne College (Lemoyne-Owen College)
3. Americans for Democratic Action
4. *Brown v. Board*
5. *Plessy v. Ferguson*
6. Busing for integration
7. Junior Bar Associations
8. 14th Amendment
9. Departments of public instruction
10. Freedom Schools
11. Individual school enrollment by ethnic background in your city/state
12. Chapter 220
13. White flight
14. Milwaukee Parental Choice Program
15. School choice programs and the inclusion of parochial schools
16. Open enrollment
17. School vouchers and tuition tax credits
18. State funding for school integration in your state today
19. Segregated schools and achievement scores in your city/state
20. Resegregation efforts in today's educational arena

References

Aukofer, F. (2007). *City with a chance: A case history of civil rights revolution*. Milwaukee: Marquette University.

Civil rights activists campaign against de facto segregation in Milwaukee schools, 1964–1966 (n.d.). Swarthmore College. Retrieved from http://nvdatabase.swarthmore.edu/content/civil-rights-activists-campaign-against-de-facto-segregation-milwaukee-schools-1964-1966

Dougherty, J. (2004). *More than one struggle: The evolution of Black school reform in Milwaukee*. Chapel Hill, NC: University of North Carolina.

Kava, Russ (2009). Informational paper 28: School integration (Chapter 220) aid. Wisconsin Legislative Fiscal Bureau. Retrieved from https://docs.legis.wisconsin.gov/misc/lfb/informational_papers/january_2009/0028_school_integration_chapter_220_aid_informational_paper_28.pdf

Lloyd A. Barbee Papers (n.d.). Wisconsin Historical Society. Retrieved from http://digital.library.wisc.edu/1711.dl/wiarchives.uw-whs-mil00016

Milwaukee, Wisconsin: The Selma of the North (2010). *Black Thursday*. Retrieved from http://www.blackthursday.uwosh.edu/milwaukee.html

Miner, B. (2013a). *Lessons from the heartland: A turbulent half-century of public education in an iconic American city*. New York: The New Press.

Miner, B. (2013b). Honor Lloyd Barbee—by more than naming a school after him. *Milwaukee Journal-Sentinel*. Retrieved from http://archive.jsonline.com/blogs/purple-wisconsin/189709431.html

Ranney, J. and Aldridge-White, M. (2004). Lloyd Barbee: Fighting segregation root and branch. *Wisconsin Lawyer*, 7(4). Retrieved from http://www.wisbar.org/newspublications/wisconsinlawyer/pages/article.aspx?Volume=77&Issue=4&ArticleID=740

Ranney, J. A. (n.d.). Wisconsin court system, history of the courts, articles on Wisconsin legal history: Attorney Lloyd Barbee. Wisconsin Court System. Retrieved from https://www.wicourts.gov/courts/history/article47.htm

Richards, E. and Mulvaney, L. (2014). 60 years after *Brown v. Board of Education* intense segregation returns. *Milwaukee Journal-Sentinel*. Retrieved from http://archive.jsonline.com/news/education/60-years-after-brown-v-board-of-education-intense-segregation-returns-b99271365z1-259682171.html

Wisconsin Legislative Fiscal Bureau (2005). School integration (Chapter 220) aid: Informational paper. Retrieved from https://docs.legis.wisconsin.gov/misc/lfb/informational_papers/january_2005/0028_school_integration_chapter_220_aid_informational_paper_28.pdf

CONCLUSION

What Have We Learned About Uncovering Lesser-Known Heroes?

"They spoke truth to power and attempted reasoned solution to an oppressive situation."
—Author

Opening doors is a difficult thing. When the doors have been bolted for centuries, it becomes nearly impossible. When the many push on the door, indeed pound the door with a mighty force, and the door still doesn't open, the many tend to drop away in despair. The few stay on to challenge the door. These have been stories of some of the few. It is not to say that there weren't thousands of more such people as described in this book—tens of thousands of more. It is to say that perhaps the icons in social justice, the big movements, and the political machines slowly then powerfully created and grew the national momentum for equality in America, but it is at the local levels where actions cause change. Collective local actions, such as depicted in these stories told in this volume, have enduring outcomes that spiral into national change and cause inroads to thinking regarding oppression and inequality. The large-scale change results from the reality that at the same times in different locations across the nation local leaders together with citizens, or in many cases local individuals acting alone, rise to challenge the oppressive status quo and make a mark on inequality. This mark expands to the masses and begins a journey of its own far beyond one local level. The momentum begun by local activists carries to national prominence and creates a change in dominant culture perspective. The shift in thinking, combined with continued attention from a now larger base of activists from many sections of the country, slowly turns the wheels of progress so that the distance from the past toward the future can be traveled in such a way as to attempt to repair the past and hope for the future.

We see this in the story of Caroline Quarlls as she refuses to accept the punishment doled out to her by her slave master. She feels the oppression acutely and knows she cannot live a life in bondage to others. With great courage and ingenuity, she strikes out alone amid horrific danger to seek the freedom she knows she deserves. Taking chance after frightening chance, she realizes along the journey that she is not alone. Surely, there are those who would hurt her; yet, there are others who would help her. Indeed, as she escapes to freedom many others are gathered to protect her and to conceal her and who later spread the story of her success for others to duplicate. These people grow in their numbers as she pursues her freedom while avoiding arrest. Because Caroline decided to flee oppression many see her fate and understand the reasons for it. They see and experience the injustice. They are led by Caroline, one individual, to consider and act upon a higher ground. By and large and near and far Caroline's story inspires others. The inspiration is not just to run but to perceive the reasons for running and to join in the larger-than-one-person's-run struggle to end the necessity for anyone to run.

Similarly, we can see in the case of Joshua Glover that the common folk of the city of Milwaukee refuse the injustice of oppression. Glover has left his owner and believes he is a free man because he is living in what has been termed a free state. He becomes well liked and self-sufficient. He hones his trade and contributes to the local economy. He is content. Although Glover has found his peace and more freedom than he could ever have hoped for, he is betrayed by a person who is looking to profit by his capture and arrest. The result is that Glover is hunted down like an animal, beaten, chained, and carried away to a cage called jail. There he is kept against his will for a trial he didn't deserve, like so many others before him and like so many others after him. His fate would be doomed except for the local citizenry and its leaders who relentlessly seek lawful methods of extricating Glover from his situation. The authorities in power stiff-arm every tactic used by the citizens to legally release Glover and dodge the legal issues brought forth. Their racism and oppressive natures are evident. Still, repeatedly citizens meet in small groups and in complete community assembly to hold vigil on Glover's safety and to discuss methods of thwarting the injustice they feel for Glover. At one point, even citizens from a nearby community arrive to help the crusade to end the discrimination. When all else fails, the citizens feel they have no choice but to take action themselves to open the jail and send Glover away to freedom. The citizens in this case had done what so many other citizens across the nation had done. They spoke truth to power and attempted reasoned solution to an oppressive situation. And like so many other cases across the nation their efforts were stalled, delayed, and denied. It may be said that citizens ought not to take the law into their own hands; however, what progress would be made if this never happened? Standing up for freedom can be messy, daunting, and difficult; yet, if citizens like those in the Glover case do not stand up for freedom, hope for a better future cannot be expected. Joshua Glover was no martyr. He was one story on the road to freedom.

The establishment of African American women's clubs shows just how widespread social injustice can be. It also shows how organized and effective groups of people can be at both local and state levels in eradicating an unwanted social disease. It is an amazing and complex story that requires decades of time and hundreds of people to unfold. Yes, there are key leaders at state levels who bring their cause to the national forum; however, local small (sometimes tiny) women's clubs play the key role not only in forming themselves but especially in networking with each other to create a larger state thrust which eventually results in national momentum. And though the majority of White women of the time kept hold of the idea of the oppression of Black women, at the same time they were aware of their own subordinate status in American society. White women's clubs were established for many reasons and one of the primary purposes was to establish civil rights and privileges for equal citizenship and treatment of White women. It became apparent to White women that they felt a unique and common bond with Black women in that both groups were oppressed regarding gender status. White women still resisted the association with Black women, but as time went on the value of integration became evident to enhance the cause of the gender. White women's suffrage movements as early as the 1840s lead years later in the 1860s and 1870s to eventually consider the inclusion of Black women. Meanwhile, Black women had also been forming community clubs. These clubs, beginning as early as the 1830s, focused on child rearing, education, and moral justice; however, of course, Black women wanted all the same rights as White women who, in turn, wanted all the same rights as White men. The point is that the Black women's clubs resonated with White women's clubs as a gender-specific population oppressed by the masses because of their gender.

Both Black and White women's clubs were working in the same ways but separately, each to achieve the same goal—social equality. It was inevitable that they would begin to work together toward the common goal. Indeed, they did and this unique perspective on a freedom movement slowly evolved over decades to a point in the 1890s at which all women pledged to help each other in a *Lifting As We Climb* fashion toward equality. By this time, thousands, perhaps tens of thousands, of Black and White women and men had joined forces to form a new vehicle for equality. The individuals who put together small groups of concerned citizens which networked with other small groups of concerned citizens to form a state thrust for equality created the national movements and their leaders who drove the momentum to repair the past and hope for a better future.

By the time we get to the story of Ezekiel Gillespie it is easy to see that, without ever wanting to downplay the well-organized, well-orchestrated, and effective all-Black systems of freedom fighting, working toward social justice, civil rights, and equality was often an integrated undertaking. It would be easy to say that Gillespie hitched his wagon to the star Alexander Mitchell who provided the means and the motivation to begin a local "street corner" group to start a movement, but, as the chapter argues, Gillespie was known to work alone toward civil rights issues, in particular suffrage, and there is no evidence that Mitchell was a part of the Milwaukee Seven. It may be more accurate to say that Gillespie was a pawn in the hands of local White lawyers who for their own reasons sought Black suffrage. However, again as the chapter argues, this notion meets with reasonable arguments which conclude that Gillespie was not merely a pawn. His lack of recognition for the part he played indeed may be self-imposed for logical reasons. Only a mere handful of people were aware of Gillespie's involvement even though the resulting court case bears his name. His family for years never knew. This tells us that sometimes, perhaps often, uncovering the real heroes of social justice and equality becomes nearly impossible or at least very difficult. This may be because actions were not meant to be based on individuals, but, rather, they were meant to be based on the entire milieu of events unfolding in unison to form lifelines for freedom. Anonymity became important so that plans and actions, current and future, had a better chance to succeed. From this, we can conclude that we will never uncover all the pivotal local leaders and citizens who made the progress so far. However, we know they were there. Ezekiel Gillespie's story tells us.

The last two chapters of the book take place at roughly the same time. It is a time in which activism is at its peak across America. Once again, we see local activists, who may or may not be inspired by national icons, creating and developing plans to demand a level playing field. And once again, we see the local actions impacting state leaders and the status quo so that not just awareness but action on both local and state levels occurs. As the chapters point out, local activism gained media attention from around the country in such degrees that other communities were bolstered in their own attempts to establish equality and were inspired to continue. This tactic of gaining media attention and coverage became a crucial factor in uniting activists from many parts of America and for creating support and momentum to carry on the activism intended to create change. Media was a new factor and a powerful one. It became arguably the primary factor in creating change. Beginning as early as the 1940s, the push for fair housing and unemployment increased as the struggle for equal education plodded on. By the 1950s, local leaders such as Father Groppi, Vel Phillips, and Lloyd Barbee were active both in the courts and on the streets. Groppi and Phillips focused on fair housing and employment. Barbee focused on education. Countless meetings and presentations with and to city officials, especially the city council, and school officials, especially the school board, were held at which evidence of discrimination was offered and plans for corrections were shared. After literally years of reasoned articulation, discussion, and persuasion, city and school officials continued to stiff-arm and undermine every avenue brought forth. The mayor and important state officials did the same. By the 1960s, citizen's groups such as the Milwaukee United School Integration Committee (MUSIC), the National Association for the Advancement of Colored People (NAACP), the NAACP Milwaukee Youth Council, the local chapter of the Congress on Racial Equality (CORE), and many others had formed. After years of frustration, these groups now resorted to overt activism with special focus on media attention to gain state-wide and nation-wide recognition of the injustices they experienced and the solutions they offered. Sit-ins, marches, demonstrations, public speeches, bus blocking, construction chaining, and any other nonviolent measure that could be taken were used to draw media and thus the state and the nation to their causes. Local politicians were called out and asked to explain their actions and their votes. Explanations for why these politicians resisted efforts to equalize housing, employment, and education were demanded. Peaceful confrontation was common place with activists purposely avoiding violence, which, of course, inevitably resulted in the long run. Though Groppi, Phillips, and Barbee had settled on different issues on which to focus, in reality everybody struggled for every issue. As Groppi and Phillips marched and continued to challenge city hall, Barbee did actual studies of racial inequality and continued to challenge the local school board. As throughout history, the oppressed were threatened by the oppressors. Peaceful activism exploded into violence and resulted in citizen and even police brutality. As throughout history, speaking truth to power resulted in punishment, injury, and continued discrimination/oppression. Still, Father Groppi would join with Vel Phillips to finally reach a local fair housing ordinance that would later become the state model, and Lloyd Barbee filed and dedicated himself to arguably the most important landmark federal court case in the history of school desegregation—one that changed state law and that had impact and repercussions throughout America. Again, we see the connection between everyday local people doing what they believe is right to end oppression (at great risk and personal sacrifice) and state and national effects of their work. In this way, the premise fits: *The more we uncover local individuals who risked their lives to repair the past and hope for a better future, the more we see that national civil rights movements gained their success and notoriety on the backs of local heroes.*

SELECTED COURT DECISIONS REGARDING DISCRIMINATION BASED ON ETHNICITY

- *Prigg v. Pennsylvania* (1842)
- *Dred Scott* (1857)
- *Slaughterhouse Cases* (1873)
- *United States v. Cruikshank* (1876)
- *United States v. Reese* (1876)
- *Strauder v. West Virginia* (1880)
- *Plessy v. Ferguson* (1896)
- *Williams v. Mississippi* (1898)
- *Cumming v. Richmond County Board of Education* (1899)
- *Guinn v. United States* (1915)
- *Nixon v. Herndon* (1927)
- *Nixon v. Condon* (1932)
- *Powell v. Alabama* (1932)
- *Grovey v. Townsend* (1935)
- *Breedlove v. Suttles* (1937)
- *Gaines v. Canada* (1938)
- *New Negro Alliance v. Sanitary Grocery Co.* (1938)
- *Lane v. Wilson* (1939)
- *Chambers v. Florida* (1940)

- *Smith v. Allwright* (1944)
- *Korematsu v. United States* (1944)
- *Morgan v. Virginia* (1946)
- *Shelley v. Kraemer* (1948)
- *McLaurin v. Oklahoma State Regents* (1950)
- *Sweatt v. Painter* (1950)
- *Henderson v. United States* (1950)
- *Brown v. Board of Education* (1954)
- *Hernandez v. Texas* (1954)
- *Lucy v. Adams* (1955)
- *Browder v. Gayle* (1956)
- *NAACP v. Alabama* (1958)
- *Gomillion v. Lightfoot* (1960)
- *Boynton v. Virginia* (1960)
- *Garner v. Louisiana* (1961)
- *Bailey v. Patterson* (1962)
- *Baker v. Carr* (1962)
- *McLaughlin v. Florida* (1964)
- *New York Times Co. v. Sullivan* (1964)
- *Harper v. Virginia State Board of Elections* (1966)
- *South Carolina v. Katzenbach* (1966)
- *Heart of Atlanta Motel, Inc. v. United States* (1964)
- *Loving v. Virginia* (1967)
- *Jones v. Mayer Co.* (1968)
- *Green v. School Board of New Kent County* (1968)
- *Griggs v. Duke Power Co.* (1971)
- *Swann v. Charlotte-Mecklenburg Board of Education* (1971)
- *Gates v. Collier* (1974)
- *Milliken v. Bradley* (1974)
- *Village of Arlington Heights v. Metropolitan Housing Development Corp.* (1977)
- *University of California Regents v. Bakke* (1978)
- *Batson v. Kentucky* (1986)
- *Adarand Constructors, Inc. v. Peña* (1995)
- *Grutter v. Bollinger* (2003)
- *Schuette v. Coalition to Defend Affirmative Action* (2014)

SELECTED COURT DECISIONS REGARDING DISCRIMINATION BASED ON GENDER

- Muller v. Oregon (1908)
- Adkins v. Children's Hospital (1923)
- Pittsburgh Press Co. v. Pittsburgh Commission on Human Relations (1937)
- Griswold v. Connecticut (1965)
- Phillips v. Martin Marietta Corp. (1971)
- Reed v. Reed (1971)
- Eisenstadt v. Baird (1972)
- Frontiero v. Richardson (1973)
- Roe v. Wade (1973)
- Cleveland Bd. of Ed. v. LaFleur (1974)
- Stanton v. Stanton (1975)
- Craig v. Boren (1976)
- Meritor Savings Bank v. Vinson (1986)
- Johnson v. Transportation Agency (1987)
- Oncale v. Sundowner Offshore Serv., Inc. (1987)
- International Union, UAW v. Johnson Controls, Inc. (1991)
- Franklin v. Gwinnett County Public Schools (1992)
- J.E.B. v. Alabama ex rel. T.B. (1994)
- Faragher v. City of Boca Raton (1998)

- *Davis v. Monroe County Board of Education* (1999)
- *Miller v. Albright* (1999)
- *US v. Morrison* (2000)
- *Nguyen v. INS* (2001)
- *Pennsylvania State Police v. Sudors* (2003)
- *Burlington Northern and Santa Fe Railway Co. v. White* (2006)

Peter Lang PRIMERS
in Education

Peter Lang Primers are designed to provide a brief and concise introduction or supplement to specific topics in education. Although sophisticated in content, these primers are written in an accessible style, making them perfect for undergraduate and graduate classroom use. Each volume includes a glossary of key terms and a References and Resources section.

To order, please contact our Customer Service Department:
- 800-770-LANG (within the US)
- 212-647-7706 (outside the US)
- 212-647-7707 (fax)

To find out more about this and other Peter Lang book series, or to browse a full list of education titles, please visit our website:
www.peterlang.com

Published primers include:

- *Critical Pedagogy* (1st and 2nd editions) by Joe L. Kincheloe
- *Critical Constructivism* by Joe L. Kincheloe
- *Foucault and Education* by Gail McNicol Jardine
- *Literacy Primer* by Brett Elizabeth Blake & Robert W. Blake
- *Standards* by Raymond A. Horn, Jr.
- *Mentorship* by Carol A. Mullen
- *Piaget and Education* by David W. Jardine
- *Popular Culture* (1st and rev. editions) by John A. Weaver
- *Teaching Writing* by P.L. Thomas
- *John Dewey* by Douglas J. Simpson
- *No Child Left Behind* by Frederick M. Hess & Michael J. Petrilli

- *Self-Study of Teaching Practices* by Anastasia P. Samaras & Anne R. Freese
- *Authentic Assessment* by Valerie J. Janesick
- *Bakhtin* by Carolyn M. Shields
- *American Public Education Law* (1st, 2nd, and 3rd editions) by David C. Bloomfield
- *History of American Education* by David Boers
- *Standardized Testing* by Richard P. Phelps
- *Feminist Theories and Education* by Leila E. Villaverde
- *Studying Urban Youth Culture* by Greg Dimitriadis
- *Action Research* by Patricia H. Hinchey
- *Pedagogy* by Philip M. Anderson
- *Race and Education* by Aaron David Gresson III
- *Rethinking Technology in Schools* by Vanessa Elaine Domine
- *Social Theory in Education* by Philip Wexler
- *Aesthetics* by Boyd White
- *Vygotsky on Education* by Robert Lake
- *Peace and Pedagogy* by Molly Quinn
- *Transformative Leadership* by Carolyn M. Shields
- *History of American Higher Education* by Margaret Cain McCarthy
- *Charter School* by Anne Marie Tryjankowski
- *Civic Youth Work* by Ross Velure Roholt & Michael Baizerman
- *Arts-Based Research* by James Haywood Rolling, Jr.

www.ingramcontent.com/pod-product-compliance
Lightning Source LLC
Chambersburg PA
CBHW061350300426
44116CB00011B/2068